RE-IMAGINING THE INDUS

Mapping Media Reportage in India and Pakistan

Samir Saran

Hans Rasmussen Theting

Observer Research Foundation
New Delhi

Lahore University of Management Sciences
Lahore

KW Publishers Pvt Ltd
New Delhi

Observer Research Foundation is a public policy think-tank that aims to influence formulation of policies for building a strong and prosperous India. ORF pursues these goals by providing informed and productive inputs, in-depth research and stimulating discussion. The Foundation is supported in its mission by a cross-section of India's leading public figures, academics and business leaders.

KWW

KW Publishers Pvt Ltd
4676/21, First Floor, Ansari Road, Daryaganj, New Delhi 110002
E knowledgeworld@vsnl.net **T** +91.11.23263498 / 43528107
www.kwpub.com

ISBN 978-93-80502-96-0

Contents

Acknowledgements

We are grateful to the Lahore University of Management Sciences (School of Humanities, Social Sciences & Law) for providing research inputs and observations, Mr. Akhilesh B. Variar for his valuable participation in the coding process and research, and Ms Sonali Mittra for research assistance.

Preface

Water will arguably be one of the most critical themes in South Asian political debates in the years to come. Although the water sharing debate, especially between India and her neighbouring countries, has been one of the key issues in the region since 1947, several recent developments indicate that the emerging scarcity due to the growing demand for water will place this resource at the centre of regional politics. In this scenario, any heightened awareness of managing and sharing this precious resource is beneficial; besides, there is also the fear that in the emergent political narrative, the importance and relevance of some core aspects may be neglected. These include: the inter-relationships between changing weather patterns and water availability; agriculture, irrigation and electricity; electricity, energy policy and water; and most significantly, the relationship between communities, water bodies, development policies and lifestyles. The discussions around the politics of water must be able to accommodate some of these crucial micro-narratives, if they are to benefit the constituencies the discourse professes to serve.

The engagement on water between India and Pakistan was undefined at the time of Partition, but was subsequently formalised by the signing of the Indus Water Treaty in 1960. The treaty has managed to survive political tensions and conflicts between the two countries, but as the per capita water availability continues to decline, the debate is likely to intensify and the treaty is expected to face intense pressures in the days ahead. The per capita water availability in India has fallen from 1,800cu m in 2005 to 1,731 cu m in 2010. In Pakistan, the per capita water availability fell from 1,200 cu m per annum in 2005 to 1,038 cu m per annum in 2010.[1] This is around a third of what was available at the time of Partition. There is a reason to argue that the declining water availability itself may serve as the basis for new security apprehensions on both sides and the current framework for managing the resource may have its limitations.

The scarcity of such a critical resource could make people and policy-makers respond irrationally, leading to deepening of contests and conflicts. Water is a flammable issue that can easily be exploited by rogue organisations, terror groups and state actors, as well as by political forces to fuel hatred and conflict – phenomena witnessed around the world and in the region. The objective of this paper is to contribute an articulate, sensitive and cooperative framework to the debates on water and add a unique perspective to the growing narratives around water.

In an attempt to map the debate on water within and between Pakistan and India, this monograph has chosen to analyse news reports in the two countries during the spring and winter months of 2010 by deploying Media Content Analysis (MCA). Mapping and measuring the intensity and characteristics of the debate will hopefully help politicians, policy-makers and scholars to identify the pressure points and help to focus their response as well. Another objective of the research is to relocate the water debate from the arena of myths and perceptions, into a conversation based on existing facts. What is actually driving the debate on water? How is the discussion on water framed in the media and which of the causes and consequences of water scarcity receive the most attention and in what time periods? Media is a vital component of public opinion formation and studying media coverage on this vital issue will help understand how people, policy-makers and nations imagine 'water' and its nuances.

Key Findings

- Agricultural concerns and inter-provincial disputes dominate media reportage in Pakistan.
- Indian media lays greater emphasis on urban water concerns and interventions, including groundwater and domestic consumption.
- There is a seasonal lag between India and Pakistan as the media of both these countries is sensitive to the actions and criticisms of each other. India figures high in Pakistani press reports during winter months, while Pakistan only appears in Indian reports during spring months.
- Level of hostility towards India remains relatively low and reduces significantly over the two seasons in the media reportage in Pakistan.
- The criticism of the Indus Waters Treaty (IWT) has been relatively moderate and sober in the media space.
- Lack of sensitivity to changing climate, environmental degradation and agriculture practices is apparent in both the Indian and Pakistani media.
- There is an equal emphasis on the aspects of water governance and infrastructure in both the countries.
- Media reports in both the countries, Pakistan more than India, recognise the need for the two countries to cooperate on water issues.

Introduction

Public opinion on issues of significance is often a product of debate in the public sphere. While there are contrary viewpoints on the strength of the relationship between media discourse and public opinion and on the sequencing within this relationship, there is an acceptance that they do closely follow each other. The conversations around water should cover three key elements even at a cursory level. The first and the most dominant is the political nuance and how it seemingly continues to dominate media and research space. The second element that is gaining importance is water governance with associated discussions on infrastructure, administration and management. The third and the most recent narrative places water firmly within the discourse on climate. This section will briefly discuss each of these elements in relation to India and Pakistan.

The Political Discourse

The Indus water debate has taken different forms, with a broad division into conflict, cooperation and conciliation. Within each of these aspects lie subsets of discourses which have taken different directions over the years. The debate has evolved from its beginning in 1952, when the discussion was characterised by the presence of external actors with an intended depoliticised focus. David Lilienthal, former chairman of Tennessee Valley

Authority, who is widely recognised as having begun the mediation process, and former World Bank President, Eugene R. Black, argued that the issue (of water-sharing between India and Pakistan) was to be treated as a functional or an engineering problem rather than a political one.[2] N.D. Gulhati, who led the Indian delegation in the IWT negotiations, supports this position obliquely, while describing the mood during the negotiations in the 1950s: "There was no mass audience to address nor rhetoric or inflammatory debating tactics"[3] – reaffirming the technical nature of the endeavour at that time.

Contesting this view and the proposition that the IWT of 1960 was devoid of political contestations, the head of Pakistan's Indus Water Commission, Jamaat Ali Shah later stated, "In 1960, Pakistan did not want to give its three rivers to India". He further argued that India had breached water agreements and that this would jeopardise the water treaty. He noted that the countries should look beyond the treaty in any future negotiations.[4] On the other hand, Shah's Indian counterpart, G. Ranganathan, maintained that both sides were committed to the treaty and that 'all hydropower projects being built by India conform to the provisions of the IWT'.[5] This, in a sense, highlights how the stakeholders have comprehended the treaty differently and from their disparate vantage points.

The water debates soon after transformed into risk discourses and the IWT came to be viewed through the lens of security. John Briscoe, former senior adviser to the World Bank on water issues with specific experience on Indo-Pakistan relations, wrote: 'This (downstream) vulnerability was driven home when India chose to fill Baglihar exactly at the time when it would impose maximum harm on farmers in downstream Pakistan...", adding "...once it has constructed all of the planned hydropower plants on the Chenab, India will have an ability to effect major damage on Pakistan." His assertions were a reflection of a belief that the IWT offered an "uneven playing field...the regional hegemon is the upper riparian and has all the cards in its hands. This asymmetry means that it is India which is driving the train, and that change must start from here."[6] In an interview with Pakistani Newspaper, *The Dawn*, Briscoe added the narrative of terror to the security discussion and asserted: "If you want to give Lashkar-e-Tayyeba and other Pakistani militants an issue that really rallies people, give them water".[7] This perception of the water-sharing framework is undoubtedly an extreme political reading of the issue that may find resonance in some quarters.

The apprehension of 'water wars' between India and Pakistan has been a prevailing issue of concern to which Briscoe alludes to as well. Undala Z. Alam, however, differs from this line of thought and avers, "The issues of water scarcity, competitive use and a wider conflict do not necessarily lead to war, since war cannot guarantee a country's water supply in the long run.....that India and Pakistan did not wage war over the Indus waters despite prime candidacy for a water war, leads to the questioning of the water wars rationale..." She further adds that the rationale is based upon three principal factors: water scarcity, a wider conflict and bellicose public statements – none of these has met the 'conflict situation' barometer.[8]

Surprisingly, in a rare statement widely perceived by the Indian side as vindicating its stand, former Pakistan Foreign

Minister S. M. Qureshi admitted that the Pakistani authorities had a tendency to "pass the buck" and exaggerate differences with India over the sharing of river waters. According to Qureshi, mismanagement within the country itself resulted in the loss of 34 million-acre feet of water,[9] a fact that accentuates the importance of governance and management of the resource and shifts the emphasis from the political. Ramaswamy Iyer, former secretary of the Water Resources Ministry of India, has continually emphasised the need to define the 'water issue' conceptually. He has argued that the 'issue' of 'water-sharing' has been resolved by the IWT and now the two countries must look for constructive cooperation in implementing the treaty in its letter and spirit and manage this resource even while dealing with emerging challenges such as climate change.[10]

Governance

Water management has emerged as one of the most critical factors in the debate as a result of plummeting per capita water availability in both the countries, with India doing only marginally better in this respect. The issue is seen to be more critical for Pakistan, given its single river system and a predominantly agricultural economy.

In a study done in 2009,[11] Michael Kugelman[12] establishes the centrality of water management to the debate in Pakistan. The report describes how intensive irrigation and poor drainage practices have caused water-logging and soil salinity throughout Pakistan. The recommendations place considerable emphasis on the development of an ecologically sustainable water infrastructure model, a balance of centralisation and decentralisation in water management and the involvement of the private sector. A considerable section of the report focuses on the inter-provincial rivalry, especially between Sindh and Punjab, with allegations of the latter drawing more than its share of water than the quota allocated by the 1991 Indus Water Sharing accord. The report quotes Kaiser Bengali, a Pakistan based economist, who asserts, "Pakistan cannot address its water crisis without a paradigm shift in the way Pakistan thinks about water management". Bengali argues for a 'socio-centric' approach which relies on physical and human resource management for a more resource efficient and ecologically conducive method, as opposed to the existing 'techno-centric' approach which focuses on engineering solutions and storage.

According to Wilson John, Pakistan's per capita storage capacity is only 150 cu m compared to 5,000 cu m in the US and Australia and 2,200 cu m in China. The holding capacity of the existing reservoirs and dams in Pakistan is 30 days, while it is between 120 to 220 days in India, 500 days in South Africa and 900 days in the US.[13] The Pakistan Vision 2030 report, published by the Planning Commission of Pakistan, states that mismanagement has caused stagnation and degradation of water sources. It also refers to the lack of storage facilities as a major challenge.[14]

Water management has also been of considerable concern in India. The mid-term appraisal of the Eleventh Plan, brought forth by the Planning Commission in 2010, recognises this challenge. The Plan expects the challenge to intensify due to rising population and growth in agricultural and industrial demand. Along with the traditional issues of pollution and inadequate efficiency of surface water irrigation, it highlights the groundwater situation as critical and cites a NASA Gravity Recovery and Climate Experiment (GRACE) satellite study indicating an alarming decrease in the level of the groundwater table.[15] The situation is particularly critical in urban centres. It is estimated that the water loss due to theft, aging pipelines and infrastructure in Mumbai is as high as 40% to 50%,[16] which places considerable stress on the resource as a whole. This is a reality experienced by all metros in India.

The report further cites that the net irrigated area through canals [in India] has actually undergone a decline, rather than achieving an accelerated growth. From an average contribution to national irrigated area (NIA) of around 17.5 million ha in the mid-1990s, area irrigated by canals has come down to less than 15 million ha in the first decade of the 21st century. A major problem affecting irrigation systems in the states is the severe erosion of the financial health of water utilities as a result of low water charges and poor recovery mechanisms. Not only does this encourage inefficient use of water and a tendency for head-end canal users to shift to water-intensive crops, it also creates an environment in which irrigation charges do not even cover the operating cost, leading to progressive neglect of maintenance and reduced efficiency. The Planning Commission Deputy Chairman, Montek Singh Ahluwalia, recently stated that the water crisis is more serious than the energy crisis in India and better pricing of water would become imperative.[17] Pricing and water-use indeed places people, practices and sustainability firmly within the water debate.

People, Practice and Environment

The danger of treating water management as an engineering solution (as was the approach in the 1950s and '60s) is that it results in neglecting the organic nature of water and its symbiotic relationship with people, life and livelihood. Consequently, we not only lose the ability to share this resource equitably, but are also prone to carelessness in its preservation. The most serious threat to water reserves in India and Pakistan is from pollution and salinity of water sources. John points out: "In India, regular groundwater quality monitoring carried out by the Ministry of Water Resources has shown high incidence of arsenic, fluoride and iron in certain inland and coastal areas. The problem of salinity has been increasingly noticed in the coastal areas of Tamil Nadu, Gujarat, Orissa and Pondicherry. The inland presence of salinity has been detected consistently in Maharashtra, Punjab, Rajasthan, Haryana, Gujarat, Karnataka, Uttar Pradesh, Delhi, Orissa and Bihar. The high levels of salinity are caused by excessive exploitation of groundwater and surface water".[18] The problem becomes more complex as close to 90% of the rural population of India uses groundwater for drinking and household purposes.[19]

The problem of groundwater pollution is also prevalent in Pakistan. In the state of Punjab, drinking water supplied to 11 cities with a population of over 2 million was found to be laced with excess arsenic and fluoride concentrations. In addition to this, it is estimated that 36% of the population of Sindh and Punjab was exposed to high (five times the safe limit) arsenic levels in the water. Drinking water in several urban areas of Pakistan has also been shown to be laced with biological and chemical pollutants, mainly because 99% of industrial effluent and 92% of urban waste water are discharged into rivers without treatment.

The changing climate is also an ever-present reality for the region. A World Bank report confirms that given the high seasonal concentration and high variability in rainfall, risks associated with climate variability were likely to increase in the entire South Asian region. It specifically cites both India and Pakistan as being affected by growing water scarcity. Even while conceding that precise consequences of the changes were hard to predict, the report indicates that the region was highly sensitive to climate change and the receding glaciers in the Hindu Kush could initially increase annual runoff in the glacial fed rivers, only to be followed by a steep decrease in annual flows.[20]

The report highlights that agricultural productivity in the region has slowed down and one of the threats most pertinent to the agricultural sector was the precarious water situation. It prescribes adaptation practices such as planting resilient crop varieties, changing planting dates and adopting farming practices with a shorter growing season. It also suggests considerable investment in research, advanced technology development and dissemination.

The report, "India's Initial National Communication to United Nations Framework Convention on Climate Change", pointed out: "The hydrological cycle, a fundamental component of climate, is likely to be altered due to climate change... preliminary assessments have revealed that the severity of droughts and intensity of floods in various parts of India is likely to increase". The report pointed out that the rise in sea levels and melting of glaciers "will adversely affect the water balance in different parts of India and quality of groundwater along the coastal plains".[21] Pakistan also faces consequences of climate change. According to John, "Pakistan could suffer serious food crises caused by flooding of its fertile areas in Punjab and other places, as it happened in 2010. Dramatic changes in monsoon patterns are likely to lower productivity".[22]

These discussions are the point of departure for this study and the three specific themes examined herein help us define the scope of Media Content Analysis (MCA) as well as frame the main research question and its sub-themes.

Research Question and Methodology

The broad research question for this paper is: What is the general discourse on water scarcity and related crises in the Indian and Pakistani media?

This study, while deploying Media Content Analysis (MCA), scrutinizes media coverage on three specific themes discussed in the previous section:

- The Political Discourse
- Water Governance
- People, Practice and Environment

The research seeks to describe media narrations on each of these core issues in the Indian and Pakistani press during the spring and winter months of 2010 and attempts to arrive at a comprehensive understanding of the discourse.

Rationale for the method used

This study employs MCA as the method to evaluate and understand the portrayal of water shortage within and between Pakistan and India in the respective media(s) of the two countries. This method will assist in bringing forth the key themes in the water debate, repetitive patterns and meaningful absences in the media coverage. The adoption of MCA lends this research two distinct advantages over any other research methodology.

The distinct ability of the MCA to analyse a large body of text would be crucial in managing the expected abundance of coverage on water issues in the mainstream media of Pakistan and India, especially if a meaningful time-frame of the research and a wide cross-section of the media are to be included in order to make the analysis more representative. This ability is widely recognised by a number of scholars and is emphasised by the assertions of Gerbner, that this method is the appropriate tool to "delineate trends, patterns and absences" across a large sample size.[23] If structured purposefully, this method has the inherent capability to draw valid inferences from a large sample size by "systematically and objectively" seeking out patterns and characteristics within a text.[24] This ability of the MCA to conduct dispassionate research is also reaffirmed by Weber[25] and Krippendorff,[26] two experts who saw great potential in this approach to media research.

Another important characteristic of this approach is its usefulness in gauging the dynamics that may surround any quantitative findings. Max Weber saw this method as a means of monitoring the 'cultural temperature' of society.[27] The study of media coverage on water issues in both countries is important because the media sets the agenda for the public debate to a large extent. Increasing water shortage in both the countries is likely to induce constraints in several areas. The potential calamity caused by the deepening water shortage will be reflected by the media. In this light, media coverage can be seen as an indicator of the general sentiments and views on the causes and consequences of water shortage. Editorial biases notwithstanding, the reporter, who is also a citizen, represents the smallest political unit in any country. The reporter's expressions in the media may offer an interesting insight into the thoughts of the country's populace on the issues under consideration; by deploying this methodology, we may be able to draw some insight into the prevailing sentiments surrounding water.

Since the discourse on water is widely seen as being political, the media is certainly used by governments and other interested parties as a means of stating positions, promoting perceptions and communicating with the citizenry and stakeholders. The MCA is a means to decipher key messages within large narrations; it is described as "the primary message-centred methodology" by Neuendorf.[28] This is one of the reasons why, "in the field of mass communication research, content analysis has found considerable favour and has been the fastest growing technique over the past 20 years or so".[29]

However, there is a debate on the extent of the effectiveness of the MCA. Some scholars firmly categorise MCA as a purely quantitative research tool and espouse "objectivity, inter-subjectivity, a priori design, reliability, validity, generalisability, replicability, and hypothesis testing" for its successful application.[30] Qualitative analysis clearly lies outside the range of this method. This inability to employ MCA for qualitative analysis is also recognised by Graber,[31] who argues: "By looking at aggregated meaning-making across texts, the method tends to skate over complex and varied processes of meaning-making within texts." Qualitative analysis is more appropriate through other methods, including discourse analysis, semiotic analysis, interpretative analysis or critical analysis,[32] although, "with only minor adjustment, many are appropriate for use in content analysis as well".[33]

Shoemaker and Reese[34] do not support the hypothesis that the usefulness of content analysis is limited to quantitative research alone. They develop two distinct approaches to MCA – the behaviourist approach and the humanist approach. While the behaviourist approach concerns itself with the effects that the content produces, the humanist approach looks backwards from media content to try to identify what it says about society and the culture producing it. The humanist approach seeks to discover 'truths' about a society by deciphering the "the media's symbolic environment".[35] This humanist approach to the MCA lends significantly to the current research and it is through this ability of the MCA that we seek to uncover the 'truths' in the public debate on water in both the countries.

Despite the strong endorsement of the MCA for use in qualitative research, our research remains careful not to predict the motivation of the producers or the interpretation of the audiences based on the MCA alone, and we agree that for this purpose a combination of methodologies would be needed. The MCA alone remains unable to engage with the deep-rooted, historic, religious and cultural biases that may be agitated within individuals on sensitive issues such as water in the Indian and Pakistani media. In our research, whenever inferences have been made from the interrogation of the texts, they are usually discussed in context or from a perspective that is transparent.

The key aspect that determines the effectiveness of the MCA is its Inter Coder Reliability (ICR). The ICR is the extent of agreement between different coders (scholars) on the inferences arrived at from the interrogation of the texts. "*If content analysts cannot demonstrate strong reliability for their findings, then people who want to apply these findings should be wary of developing implementations*".[36] The findings arrived at by different coders have the potential to be biased by the values, beliefs and specific social and political leanings of the coder.[37] In fact, the susceptibility to coder bias is the foremost disadvantage of the MCA.[38]

Some, however, see this susceptibility as a virtue of the method and argue if analysts "*were not allowed to read texts in ways different from the ways other readers do, content analysis would be pointless*".[39] In the current research, the ICR test will be tested by two coders with different educational, social and cultural backgrounds: European and Indian. The advantage of this combination is that we will be able to combine contextual knowledge with objectivity. In this study, Inter-Coder Reliability (ICR) of over 80% was achieved, where ICR=Agreement/ (Agreement+Disagreement).

Time Frame

The first variable for the MCA was the time frame for which the Pakistani and the Indian online media articles were analysed. Since the purpose was to capture the general debate on water issues in both the countries, the research steered clear of the period where Pakistan was shocked by the late summer/fall flood months of 2010. Though this period is interesting in relation to how the media coverage responds to extreme crisis, it would not create an impression of the general public debate.

In order to do this, media coverage on this issue in two different periods, the winter months (January-February-March) and the summer months (April-May-June), was analysed. The two periods were selected in an attempt to draw distinct results, with winter months being the months of water deficiency due to reduced glacial flows and the summer months being normal flow periods.

Search Terms

The overall sample data was collected from the mainstream English language Indian and Pakistani online media sources. The samples were collected using the search term "water shortage crisis" alongside "Pakistan" and "India" for the individual countries. Additionally, the archives of each source were examined where available, for water crisis related texts. The search was limited to the time frame. It must be mentioned here that the availability of data from the online news media was largely dependent on the quality and accessibility of the respective archives. This is a potential bias within MCA and could distort representation on the basis of online presence. On the other hand, it could be argued that better archives may reflect size and significance and, hence, their representation must be commensurate. Since the study is intended to provide insight into the general discourse on water, a sample set based on the most significant online newspapers was deemed appropriate.

Another weakness of the methodology is the lack of representation of the Urdu media in Pakistan and the vernacular press in India. This is primarily due to the limits of the scope of this particular research, both in time and resources. In the course of examining the media organisations, it was discovered that most mainstream Urdu and Hindi papers have corresponding English versions as well. The main themes in the Urdu and/ or vernacular media would mostly be covered in their English publications, although with certain time lead or lag. However, we acknowledge that some themes and content might have been lost due to the absence of Urdu and vernacular media that do not have corresponding English publications. This should be addressed by a longer and more comprehensive analysis of this debate.

At this stage, it must also be mentioned that there was a discussion on some of the more radical publications in Pakistan, with smaller reach and niche constituencies. The decision to not consider these was based on two factors. First, to seek the contours of the water debate in the radical press would amount to seeking the obvious. The debate would be rhetorical and would colour the attempt to discover the centrist and articulate press coverage on the subject. Secondly, if we seek to assist in the strengthening of the more sensitive narrative on water (as is the intention of the study), it is the mainstream media that is read by the policy-makers and large sections of society that needs analysis. There could be other views, but this is one of the key structural elements of this paper.

Datasets (texts) from two seasons of the media coverage in the main online English language newspapers in India and Pakistan were examined. The newspapers from which the samples were collected were based on readership. In each of the two time periods, 100 articles were identified for both the countries (total data size of 400 articles) and, thereafter, these were reduced to 50 in each period for both these countries randomly with a total data size of 200. The randomisation was done by using the software available online at www.randomizer. org.

Coding Frame

The coding frame was structured, based on the key investigations already identified and discussed in the previous section. The process of finalising the coding frame involved an iterative and interactive engagement between the co-coders and the sample texts. This was accomplished initially by testing the suitability of the queries against the sample texts themselves. Thereafter, a framework of interrogation was designed to make it uniformly applicable across the texts in the sample data. The purpose of the structure was to create an interrogative framework that could subsequently be utilised by the coders and by other scholars and which would hold true for different time periods and sample sets.

Interrogation of Texts

The sample data was then divided into four subsets of data. Two sets for the winter months, and two sets for the summer months each from the Pakistani and the Indian media. The interrogative frameworks of a total of 19 questions were presented to each article in both datasets. The questions posed to the Indian and the Pakistani media differed in a few key areas in order to keep the questions contextually relevant.

Through the MCA, we were able to identify the dominant themes in the media reportage of the two countries. We were also able to capture some significant absences from the debate in both countries. In the following sections, we will discuss the key findings from Pakistan and India separately and based on the research framework and its themes: The Political Discourse, Governance and People, Practice and Environment. When presenting the findings, the output is represented in percentage of articles that had debated the respective question. Thus, we add up the percentage and show the distribution of arguments. By only presenting the percentage of articles that agitate a certain theme gives the impression that the rest were either ambiguous or had rejected the argument. This is not the case. This approach would leave out the "not mentioned" (some times which also equates to "not applicable" or "not pertinent") and create an inaccurate picture of the distribution.

Findings

PAKISTAN

The Political Discourse

As per the MCA, the Indus Water Treaty (IWT) is not yet dominating the reportage in Pakistan. While this may not indicate an endorsement of the IWT, it could mean a low level of discontentment or critique. While 18% of the total articles debated the IWT in relation to water shortage, only 56%[40] of these articles presented the IWT as the cause of water shortage. The remaining 44% had an ambiguous approach to the argument. For the summer months, this figure reduced significantly and only 4% of the total articles debated the IWT. Although the figure is small and shows a reduced interest in this topic, all the articles argued that the IWT was unfair and one of the causes of water shortage. There was no ambiguity in the results for the summer months.

Table 1.1: Pakistani MCA – The Political Discourse

Pakistani MCA – Winter-Spring The Political Discourse		Winter (%)				Spring (%)			
		Yes	No	A*	N**	Yes	No	A*	N**
CAUSES	IWT	10	0	8	82	4	0	0	96
	Indian action and/or transgression	36	2	14	48	22	0	2	76
	Inter-provincial water distribution/ unfair implementation of domestic water sharing accord	26	0	6	68	24	0	2	72
IMPLICATIONS	Conflict between stakeholders (People, Institutions, Political Parties)	20	0	10	70	20	0	10	70
	Negative sentiments towards India	20	0	12	68	12	0	0	88
SOLUTION	Political pressure against India	18	4	16	62	10	0	10	80
	Increased cooperation between Pakistan and India	22	2	22	54	8	0	22	70
	Implementation of domestic water sharing arrangement in letter and spirit is a solution	30	0	0	70	6	0	0	94

A* = Ambiguous; N** = Not mentioned

The MCA shows that the inter-country dispute on water-sharing between Pakistan and India received greater attention during the winter months. As much as 76% of the articles in the MCA debated India's role in relation to water shortage. Of these, roughly 58% argued that Indian actions were the reason for water shortage while 2% argued that Indian actions were not responsible for water shortage in Pakistan. The remaining 16% chose an ambiguous or neutral approach to the question. In the summer months, the focus on India's role in water shortage in Pakistan plummeted to 24%. However, out of all the articles that mention India in the water debate, over 90% argue that India is the cause of the problem. The remaining 10% were ambiguous. This temporal difference in reportage may indicate a certain constituency that continues to apportion residual blame on external factors without debating other contributory factors.

From the analysis, it is evident that the inter-provincial disputes in Pakistan received significant attention and is comparable to the attention given to the bilateral dispute between India and Pakistan. In the winter months, 26% of the articles in the sample referred to inter-provincial distribution issues as the main cause of water shortage. Out of all the articles that covered this aspect, 80% reported it to be the cause of the problem. The figures remain stable over the seasons, only dropping 2% points from the previous percentage that placed inter-provincial water distribution at the heart of the problem. Out of all the articles that mentioned inter-provincial distribution in the water debate in the summer season, 90% see it as the reason for water shortage.

Another aspect that emerged from the MCA was the prevalence of conflict between stakeholders in the water debate. These "conflicts" need further clarification. In these cases, we are dealing with intra-provincial, sectoral and users versus utility conflicts. During the winter months, 30% of the articles positioned conflict between stakeholders within the water shortage narrative – 66% of which argued that water shortage is the reason for conflict among stakeholders. The figures for the summer months were similar to the winter months.

The MCA shows a significant negative sentiment in the reportage towards India during the winter months. An explanatory note should be added to this finding. When looking for negative sentiments towards India in the MCA for the Pakistani media, the coders looked for cases where the intentions of the Indian government and people were argued to be "ill-conceived" or "intentionally damaging" to Pakistan. Out of the 32% that were identified with these characteristics, 63% of the articles contained a negative sentiment towards India. The remaining 37% were more difficult to label as entirely negative, but showed signs of hostility towards India and Indians. Thus, they were labelled ambiguous. As expected, the percentage of articles that either argued or reported negative sentiment towards India and blamed India for the water shortage went down to 12% in the summer months. There was no ambiguity in these results.

Following the argument that India is the cause of the water problems in Pakistan, a large part of the media coverage on the solutions to water shortage revolved around whether political pressure on India was needed in order to solve the problem. During the winter months 38% of the media coverage debated political pressure. 18% argued or reported that there was a need to pressure India. While 16% remained ambiguous, 4% argued that there was no need for political responses or rhetoric. During the summer months, the percentage of articles that discussed this idea fell to 20%. Out of these articles, 50% agreed that political pressure was needed and the remaining 50% remained ambiguous.

The discussion on cooperation between India and Pakistan to resolve issues related to water shortage received noteworthy attention during the winter months with 46% of the articles covering this issue. Of this percentage, 48% argued that India and Pakistan should expand cooperation to solve issues; 48% of the articles remained ambiguous towards cooperation, and the remaining 4% conveyed lack of support. During the summer months, the percentage of articles that covered this aspect fell to 30%. In this period, only 26% were positive and the rest remained ambiguous.

Reflecting inter-provincial distribution of water as a cause of water shortage, 30% of the total articles during the winter months presented improved implementation of water-sharing arrangements between provinces as a solution. The reduction of this percentage during the summer months is interesting. From 30% in the winter months, the percentage of articles that focused on improved implementation of domestic water-sharing arrangements as a solution dropped to 6% in the summer months. There was no ambiguity in the results for winter months or the spring months.

Governance

The variable that received the greatest attention in the Pakistani MCA as a cause of water shortage was administrative lapses and management deficiencies. In the winter season, 44% of the articles focused on administrative lapses with relation to water shortage, with 86% arguing that administrative lapses were at the core of the problem. The remaining 14% were ambiguous. In the summer months, the figures remained relatively stable at 42%. In this time period, 90% of the articles argued that water shortage was due to administrative lapses. The remaining 10% were ambiguous.

Table 1.2: Pakistani MCA – Governance

		Winter (%)				Spring (%)			
		Yes	No	A*	N**	Yes	No	A*	N**
CAUSES	Administrative lapses or challenges at the local, regional or national level	38	0	6	56	38	0	4	58
	Insufficient water provision and storage infrastructure	20	0	0	80	14	0	0	86
SOLUTION	Improvement in Public water management	22	0	8	70	34	0	4	62
	Investment/ attention/ technology solutions to water provision and storage infrastructure	18	0	0	82	28	0	0	72

A* = Ambiguous; N** = Not mentioned

Another argument that found mention among the sample texts in the Pakistani media was the causal relationship of water shortage and lack of physical infrastructure, such as functioning storage facilities and pipelines. 20% of the articles in the winter months alluded to poor infrastructure as the cause of water shortage. All the articles that focused on water infrastructure argued that the state of the provision system was affecting water availability. For the summer months, this number dropped to 14% with no ambiguity or rejection of this claim.

Consequently, the coverage focussing on the need to improve governance received attention in the articles under analysis. During the winter months, 30% of the total reviewed articles debated the significance of governance in relation to water shortage, 73% of which argued that there was a need for improvement, while 27% remained ambiguous. During the summer months, the total percentage of articles that debated governance in relation to water shortage rose to 38%. Out of these, only 10% remained ambiguous, and 90% believed water shortage would be reduced with improved water governance.

Besides identifying the problem with physical water provision infrastructure, many articles also subscribed to the solution-involving investments in water related infrastructure. In the winter period, 18% of the total articles reviewed alluded to the need for such an investment. Interestingly, this number rose to 28% of the total articles during the summer months. There was no ambiguity or rejection of the idea in either season. Perhaps this is representative of the fact that as the debate moves to the summer and tension between provinces and countries simmer down, more time and space is available for substantive and technical aspects of water management.

People, Practice and Environment

As expected, a substantial percentage of the articles reviewed in the winter months focused on climatic variations, mostly seasonal, as the explanation for water shortage. In the winter months, 32% of the articles placed this explanation at the centre of the debate, of which 94% argued it to be the primary cause and only 6% were ambiguous. This percentage plummeted to 12 % during the summer months, with no ambiguity. This change in the overall attention may be attributed to higher volume of rainfall during the summer months.

Table 1.3: Pakistani MCA – People, Practice and Environment

		Winter (%)				Spring (%)			
		Yes	No	A*	N**	Yes	No	A*	N**
CAUSES FOR SHORTAGE	Changing climate/ rainfall conditions	30	0	2	68	12	0	0	88
CONSEQUENCES OF WATER SHORTAGE	Environmental degradation	4	0	0	96	6	0	2	92
	Underground water affected	6	0	0	94	6	0	0	94
	Agricultural/agro dependent rural sector suffered	58	0	0	42	56	0	2	42
	Domestic consumption affected	24	0	2	74	32	0	0	68
SOLUTION	Crop diversification or changing cropping patterns	2	0	0	98	4	0	0	96
	Training/awareness to improve water efficiency	10	0	0	90	4	0	0	96

A* = Ambiguous; N** = Not mentioned

There was little media space offered to the inter-relationship between water and the environment. Only 4% of the articles focused on this relationship in the winter period and each did draw a positive correlation. During the summer months, 8% of the total sample discussed this aspect, of which 75% posited a positive correlation and 25% were ambiguous.

The limited focus on groundwater resources in the Pakistani media was surprising. Water shortage and its effect on groundwater sources has been a concern among experts, but this is not reflected in the public debate. During the winter months, only 6% of the articles focused on the effect on groundwater sources. This percentage did not change during the summer months which reflects a low level of debate on this aspect in the main media discourse.

The concern on the consequences of water shortage is evident from the analysis. During the winter months, 58% of the articles focussed on the effect of water shortage on the agricultural sector. All of which argue that the sector would suffer from water shortage. The percentage focusing on this relationship remained stable at 58% during the summer months, though with a small change in the percentage that affirmed that it led to the agricultural sector suffering. 97% were positive and only 3% remained ambiguous. Not surprisingly, out of all the articles that mentioned water shortage and its effect on the agricultural sector, almost all contained dire predictions for the future of Pakistani agricultural sector.

The link between water shortage and reduced household consumption was mild during both seasons of analysis. During the winter months, 26% of the articles covered the effect of water shortage on household consumption. Of these articles, 92% established that reduced water availability has, in fact, lead to reduced household consumption/availability, while only 8% remained ambiguous. The percentage of articles focusing on the effect on household consumption rose to 32% during the summer months with no ambiguity. This is quite surprising as we would normally expect a reduced reportage as water is generally more abundant during the summer months.

Scant attention was given to crop diversification or agricultural innovation as a solution to water shortage. Only 2% of the articles mentioned this during the winter months, and 4% during the summer months. Although there was no ambiguity and all the articles covering crop diversification agreed on its positive effect on water efficiency, the coverage of this much discussed and well endorsed idea remains almost non-existent.

Educating farmers to use water more efficiently received some attention during the winter months. 10% of the articles argued that this could solve water shortage. However, during the summer months this plummeted to 4%. These results paint a somewhat similar picture to the earlier question. Although there was no ambiguity or rejection of the idea, the focus is still very limited in the media in comparison to its importance in 'policy-making and academic circles'.

INDIA

The Political Discourse
Expectedly, the results from the MCA for the Indian media differ in many respects from the Pakistani MCA. However,

similarities are also in abundance and these normally reflect the state of water governance, water provision and storage infrastructure. We also see important absences and differences in the debate that will be discussed in the next section.

Table 1.4: Indian MCA – The Political Discourse

		Winter (%)				Spring (%)			
		Yes	No	A*	N**	Yes	No	A*	N**
CAUSES	Unfair/or flawed IWT provisions	0	0	4	96	2	0	0	98
	Uneven inter-provincial water distribution/usage	8	0	0	92	14	0	0	86
	India not abiding by the water agreements – (Pakistan's assertion)	8	0	8	84	26	0	2	72
IMPLICATIONS	Conflict between stakeholders (People, Institutions, Political Parties)	14	0	2	84	6	0	2	92
	Pakistan accuses India of breaching water agreements	10	0	4	86	26	2	10	62
	Water is employed as a socio-political tool by extremist elements	10	0	0	90	8	0	0	92
SOLUTION	Pakistan and India should intensify cooperation to resolve water issues	10	0	0	90	12	0	12	76

A* = Ambiguous; N** = Not mentioned

On the question of whether the provision of the IWT had at any time caused water shortage in India, there was little, if any, interest in the Indian MCA. In the winter months, only 4% of the articles focused on the IWT with relation to water shortage. It is important to note that all these articles remained ambiguous to the question. During the summer months, only 2% placed the IWT within the debate. There was no ambiguity in the results during the summer months. Interestingly, it was not a very prominent discussion in the Pakistani media either at that time.

Despite the low attention given to the IWT in the Indian media, the response to Pakistan's allegations of India not abiding by the water provisions was comparatively higher over the two seasons. In the winters, 16% of the articles responded to the allegations with 8% of them labelling the assertions as unreasonable – equivalent to the number that remained ambiguous. However, during the summer months this percentage rose to 26% with only 2% remaining cryptic. Out of these articles (28%),[41] 93% labelled the allegations from Pakistan as unreasonable. The remaining 7% were ambiguous.

Like Pakistan, India also suffers from inter-provincial disputes on water-sharing. During the winter months, 8% of the total articles reviewed labelled these disputes as a central cause of water shortage. This number rose to 14% during the summer months. The results were unambiguous in both seasons and there was no rejection of the idea.

The interrogative framework for India's media reports also contained its responses to the Pakistani views of India with relation to water issues. During the winter months, 14% of the articles focused on Pakistani accusations against India and 71% of these articles reported that water shortage had lead to accusations from Pakistan that India was breaching the IWT. 29% remained ambiguous. Interestingly, the focus on Pakistani accusations against India rose to 38% during the summer months. Out of these articles, 68% showed that Pakistan had accused India of breaching water agreements, 26% were ambiguous and roughly 6% rejected the assertion.

The conflict between the different stakeholders created by water shortage was reflected in the Indian media. During the winter months, the number of articles covering tension between people, institutions and political parties was a significant 16%. Out of these articles, over 87% reported a direct connection between water shortage and conflict, and 13% remained ambiguous. As was expected, with increased availability of water during the summer months, this percentage reduced to 8%.

In addition to this, in the winter months, 10% of the articles in the MCA reported that the extremists groups in Pakistan had employed water shortage as a socio-political tool. This reduced slightly to 8% during the summer months. There was neither ambiguity nor rejection of this idea in the results.

During the winter months, 10% of the articles unambiguously argued or reported that India and Pakistan should intensify cooperation in order to solve water disputes between the two countries. This percentage is at the expected level for the Indian media. India's water problems are not argued to be caused by Pakistan; thus the articles that focused on cooperation with Pakistan do so in a broader geo-political context. During the summer months, the issue of cooperation with Pakistan was debated more frequently, and 24% of the articles mentioned this solution. Out of these articles, 50% supported the idea of cooperation with Pakistan, while the other 50% remained ambiguous.

Governance

The emphasis on governance is more prevalent in the Indian media. 38% of the total articles included this aspect in the water debate during the winter months. Out of these articles, around 68% argued that administrative lapses were the cause of water shortage. The remaining 32% were ambiguous. This percentage increased significantly during the summer months. 52% of the articles conveyed a direct linkage between administrative lapses and water shortage. Out of these articles, 92% portrayed a direct causal connection and only 8% remained ambiguous.

Table 1.5: Indian MCA – Governance

		Winter (%)				Spring (%)			
		Yes	No	A*	N**	Yes	No	A*	N**
CAUSES	Administrative lapses or challenges at the local, regional or national level	26	0	12	62	48	0	4	48
	Insufficient water/supply provision and storage infrastructure	24	0	10	66	26	0	2	72
SOLUTION	Improvement in public water management/ Regulation	24	0	12	64	32	0	2	66
	Investment in water provision/technology provision and storage infrastructure	32	0	8	60	28	0	4	68
	Public-private partnership/better water pricing partnership	2	0	0	98	4	0	0	96

A* = Ambiguous; N** = Not mentioned

The focus on insufficient physical water provision and storage infrastructure was higher in India. During the winter months, 34% of the media reports from India included this argument in the water debate. Out of these articles, 70% argued or reported that there was a direct connection, while 30% remained ambiguous. The overall attention given to the linkage between insufficient infrastructure and water shortage dropped slightly to 28% during the summer months. However, out of these articles, the percentage that portrayed a direct connection rose to 93%, while only 7% remained ambiguous.

Like in Pakistan, improving water management/regulation was an important issue. During the winter months, 36% of the articles debated water management with relation to water shortage. Out of these articles, 67% argued or reported that improving water management would help resolve water shortages, and 33% of the articles remained ambiguous. During the summer months, the overall percentage of articles debating improving water management fell slightly to 34%. However, the percentage of articles that argued or reported in the affirmative increased to 94%, with only 6% of the articles remaining ambiguous.

Improving the physical infrastructure of water provision and storage was the primary solution put forward in the Indian MCA. During the winter months, 40% of the articles took up the need for improved and enhanced water infrastructure. Out of these articles, 80% argued or reported that investment in infrastructure would solve the problem. The remaining 20% were ambiguous. During the summer months, the percentage of articles debating the need for additional water infrastructure fell to 32%, of which 88% reported or argued that investment in infrastructure would resolve water problem, while only 12% remained ambiguous.

The Indian MCA demonstrates some degree of attention to the idea of public-private partnership. During the winter months, only 2% of the articles reported or argued that this solution would help water shortage. In the summer period, the number of articles presenting this solution rose to 4%.

People, Practice and Environment

As in the analysis of the media in Pakistan, changing and variable climate did figure in the discourse on water and water scarcity. In the winter months, 28% of the articles introduced this inter-linkage between climate and water. Of this percentage, 93%[42] presented a direct linkage of climate to water shortage and only 7% remained ambiguous. As expected, this percentage dropped to 16% during the summer months. In these articles there was no ambiguity.

Table 1.6: Indian MCA – People, Practice and Environment

		Winter (%)				Spring (%)			
		Yes	No	A*	N**	Yes	No	A*	N**
CAUSES	Changing climate/ rainfall conditions	26	0	2	72	16	0	0	84
	Environmental degradation/issues	10	0	2	88	6	0	0	94
	Underground water affected	34	0	0	66	36	0	0	64
IMPLICATIONS	Agricultural/agro-dependent rural sector suffered	22	0	10	68	16	0	6	78
	Domestic consumption affected	20	0	16	64	20	0	4	76
SOLUTION	Crop diversification or changing cropping patterns	0	0	0	100	4	0	2	94
	Training/awareness to improve water efficiency	4	0	4	92	10	0	0	90

A* = Ambiguous; N** = Not mentioned

The inter-relationship of water and the environment was covered by 12% of the articles in the winter months; 83% argued or reported a correlation between water shortage and environmental degradation. The overall percentage dropped to 6% during the summer months. There was no ambiguity in this result, all of which argued or reported environmental considerations.

The issue of groundwater resources was an aspect which was reported very differently in the media texts of the two countries. In India, 34% of all the articles in the winter months covering water argued or reported that groundwater resources were depleting due to water shortage and/or increased water consumption. This percentage rose to 36% during the summer months. There was no ambiguity in the articles under analysis in either season and all portrayed a causal effect between water shortage and depleting groundwater sources.

Although the media of both the countries focused on water shortage and its effect on the agricultural sector, there was a significant difference in the scale of coverage. While Pakistan had percentages over 50 in each period, India remained around 30% or lower. During the winter months, 32% of the Indian media attention on water shortage focused on its effect on the sector. Out of these articles, less than 70% argued or reported that the agricultural sector had suffered due to water shortage, while the remaining 30% remained ambiguous. The number of articles reduced to 22% in the summer months, out of which 72% argued or reported that the agricultural sector had indeed suffered due to water shortage, while the remaining 28% was ambiguous.

Along with groundwater, it seems domestic/household consumption has taken the "missing share" from the lower reporting on agriculture (as against the Pakistani Media articles analysed) in the Indian media. In the winter months, 36% of the articles included the effect of water shortage on domestic/ household consumption, with 55% of these arguing or reporting a direct link between water shortage and consumption. The remaining 45% stayed ambiguous. During the summer months, the total number dropped to 24% with 83% conveying a direct effect on consumption. This could be reflective of the fact that the national media in India caters more to the urban realities as against the rural needs.

During the winter months no article in the MCA mentioned crop diversification as a solution to water shortage. In the summer months, however, crop diversification received some attention. Six per cent of the articles in the MCA mentioned crop diversification as a solution to water shortage. 66% reported or argued that crop diversification could be a solution, while 33% remained ambiguous.

A secondary set of solutions that were mentioned pertained to 'awareness', education and crop diversification. Some articles in the MCA brought up the idea of spreading awareness about personal water utilisation as a solution to the water problem. Another aspect of this was training farmers to use water saving techniques, etc. During the winter months, 8% of the articles debated this solution, of which 50% argued or reported that it would solve the problem, while 50% remained ambiguous. During the summer months, the percentage of articles that debated this solution rose to 10%. There was no ambiguity in the articles from this time period. All argued or reported that awareness spreading was the solution.

Analysis and Conclusion

As already discussed, the MCA is not an appropriate tool to determine the causes or motivation of how issues are reported and framed and how they are received and understood by the reader or audience. To determine these, we would need to augment the finding of the MCA with surveys and interviews at the production and reception end of the media chain. However, the results from the MCA do provide us with an overview of the current discourse on water in Pakistan and India. The findings help us acquire an insight into the distribution of focus in the debate and, thus, give an indication of the areas that frequently cause agitation, aspects that might be absent and the balance amongst the narratives.

Figure 1.1: Pakistan MCA: Key Themes

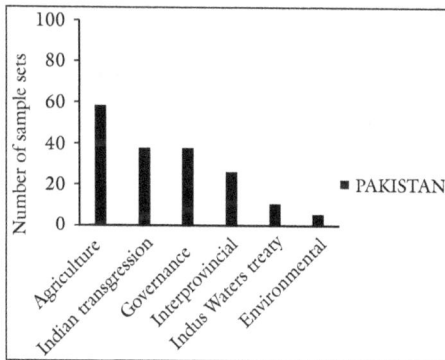

(The values presented in the graph represent the total number of articles mentioning the respective topic over the two seasons, out of a total of 100 sample sets analysed).

The MCA revealed certain basic statistics which helped in identifying the key themes in the water debate in both the countries over the two seasons. The components constituting these themes do characterise the way India and Pakistan look at the waters of the 'Indus'. It is fairly evident that agriculture, India, internal disputes, IWT and environment constitute the imagination of water by the Pakistani media. On the other hand, governance, groundwater situation, domestic consumption, agriculture and domestic water-sharing constitute the Indian media's reportage on water. There is lack of significant presence of the IWT in the samples examined. The paradox of the water discourse is that while it covers all the micro-narratives that are important, the level of debate or the sophistication of reporting on these is lacking. The level of debate can be termed as low but unambiguous. It is low as it skims over issues such as agriculture practices, environment, awareness and capacity building, but remains unambiguous as reflected in deterministic pronouncements on "controversial" issues. This is established by the fact that in the findings the "not mentioned" column is the winner, implying that expert opinions and concerns are yet to find space in the media discourse.

Figure 1.2: India MCA – Key Themes

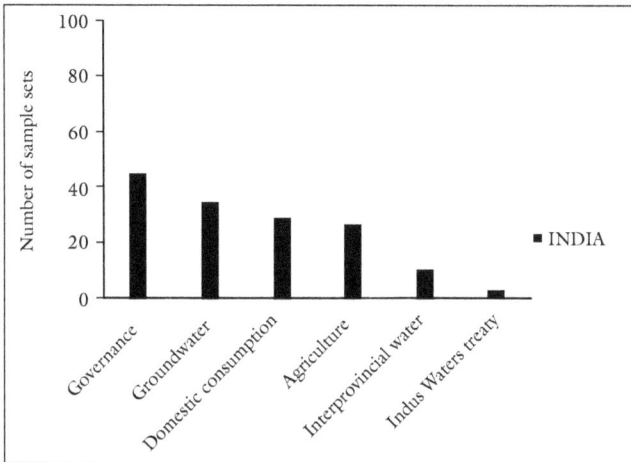

(The values presented in the graph represent the total number of articles mentioning the respective topic over the two seasons, out of a total of 100 sample sets analysed).

The above findings also show certain critical differences in the media debates of the two countries on water. While for Pakistan, Indus is synonymous with its rural needs and its relationship with India to a large extent, both these elements are subdued in the Indian debates, where water is now more of an urban theme with increased focus on issues of consumption, infrastructure and governance. This difference in our very comprehension of the waters of the shared river may lend its own dynamics to the debate. Let us briefly examine some of these distinct trends which may otherwise be overlooked when discussing the larger water narrative with its political implications.

Rural-Urban Bias

Figure 1.3: Rural-Urban Imagination of Water

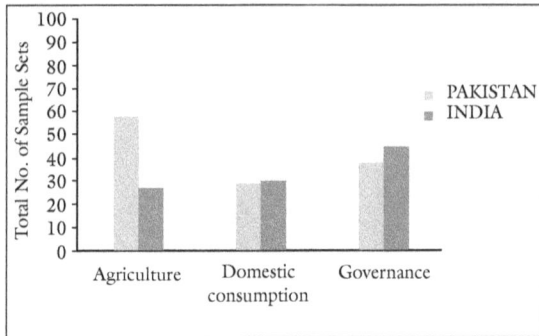

(The values presented in the graph represent the total number of articles mentioning the respective topic over the two seasons, out of a total of 100 sample sets analysed).

As stated, the water oriented interventions in India have a strong element of urban concerns and urban-centric apprehensions and interventions. These are apparent when you see the concern on domestic consumption issues and on matters of governance. It is the middle class and the elite in urban centres that are far more sensitive to matters of water management, infrastructure and governance in general. In both these aspects, the coverage is slightly more pronounced across seasons in India. On the other hand, the Pakistani media treats the rural issues with greater sensitivity, which could be attributed to its political economy that still ensures greater say of the agriculture sector in its policy-making mechanisms. This difference between the countries may form the basis of their unique approach, policies and practices around water. It also presents the debate on water sharing a nuance that would entail creating a common vocabulary to achieve efficiency in a cooperative arrangement. The needs, local political economies, lifestyles and aspirations would need to be reconciled, understood and managed.

Temporal Bias

Figure 1.4: Temporal bias in Indian and Pakistani media reportage on water issues

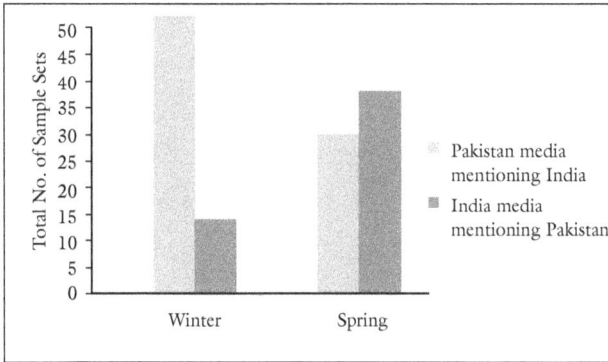

(The values presented in the graph have been calculated based on the number of articles mentioning the respective topic over the two seasons, out of a total of 50 sample sets analyzed for each)

In Pakistan, during winters, when the availability of water is low, India and Indian action come under scrutiny; and the intensity of negativity towards India reduces considerably as the water flow improves in the summer months. While the reasons for this could be many, it would be naïve to assume that political opportunism (by a section) and an attempt to deflect attention from poor governance and infrastructure do not play a significant role in the variability. Similarly in India, while the hyphenation of Pakistan and water is muted in the winter months, the awareness of the criticism from Pakistan increases in the summer months. There is a seasonal phase lag on when each of the country is sensitive to the actions and criticisms of the other. Is this witnessed due to the increased demand of electricity in the industries and homes in India that necessitates Hydro Power generation? Do our specific water requirements shape the media discourse on issues of sectoral and geographic contests? Are expediency and politics shaping the narratives in the two countries? The challenge for the two countries is clearly to focus on issues of governance without deflecting blame on politics; water should be desecuritised and depoliticised so that it remains an organic discourse about people and resources and managing needs with capabilities.

Focus on Environment

Figure 1.5: Focus on environment in India and Pakistan

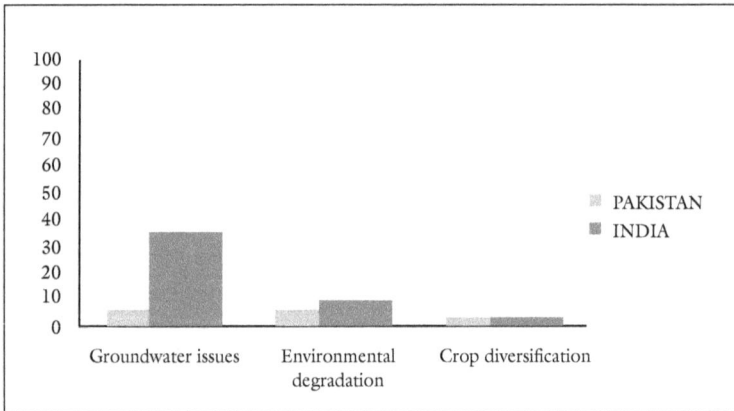

(The values presented in the graph have been calculated based on the number of articles mentioning the respective topic over the two seasons, out of a total of 100 sample sets analysed).

The third distinct trend is the apparent lack of sensitivity to changing climate, environmental degradation and agriculture practices. While in India, it may appear that there is a fair degree of concern on groundwater availability, the debate is still restricted to one on resource scarcity rather than on the ecological impact of unsustainable withdrawal. The findings show that these are the three areas which receive little attention in the reportage, even though they are vital to the life, livelihood and socio-economic development of the community and region. The neglect of more efficient agricultural practices like crop diversification and training and capacity building for the same is a symptom of the low level of debate on substantive issues. With their huge populations still growing and global warming affecting water availability and quality, India and Pakistan should begin to revisit their individual and collective discourse on this subject and this may aid in shaping a more considered collective action. The absence of these key themes in the debate, while disappointing, also do present opportunities for cooperation between the two countries. Joint Data Centres on water and Regional Environment Monitoring Station may be the appropriate next steps. Sharing of individual experiences with technologies and policies may also be possible by instituting a joint working group on this resource.

On a positive note, the MCA shows that the level of hostility towards India remains relatively low and reduces significantly over the two seasons. The periodic hostility between the two countries might have led us to expect a more aggressive discourse than what the MCA demonstrates. It is also apparent that the debate has not yet been subverted by either terror groups or by the political right in the two countries. While this is an aspect that should cause concern to both governments, dialogue and real time cooperation on managing the river may be the only way to prevent this from happening.

Lastly, the reportage on Indus Waters Treaty (IWT), another perceived area of friction and dispute, has been relatively moderate and sober and there seems to be little debate or substantive disagreement on the treaty in the media space. While we can safely infer that the provisions of the IWT are not described as unfair by the reportage, Indian action and perceived transgression is clearly a major narrative in media reports in Pakistan. This reportage suggests a level of sophistication where there seems to be a distinction between the two and this needs to be preserved. Poor implementation of the treaty by the two sides must not undermine the strength of the scheme. On the other hand, a more robust engagement mechanism around the treaty may not only strengthen it, but also improve the implementation of the provisions in letter and spirit.

The challenge is to raise the level of the debate without raising the pitch. The water narrative needs to be more informed and sensitive to some of the micro-issues that are vital. Issues of climate, crop patterns, agriculture practices, water infrastructure and use, water policy must all figure increasingly in water reportage. At the same time, to create such awareness, we must not generate hysteria and paranoia over climate, pollution or scarcity, lest these are subverted by vested interests and the narrative redeployed for political purposes.

Endnotes

1. People's Daily online, Population growth will reduce water availability in Pakistan, June 28, 2010; Available at: http://english.peopledaily.com. cn/90001/90777/90851/7042509.html
2. Kalpakian, Jack "*Identity, conflict and cooperation in international river systems*" Ashgate Publishing Ltd. 2004, p.160.
3. Gulhati, Niranjan D. "*Indus Water Treaty: An exercise in international mediation*" Bombay, Allied Publishers, 1973.
4. Shamsi, Amber Rahim "We will have to look beyond the Indus Water Treaty" *The Dawn*, March 3, 2010.
5. "*India says design of Nimo-Bazgo hydropower project is within limits*" March 29, 2010, Available online at- http://www.dnaindia.com/world/report_india-says-design-of-nimo-bazgo-hydropower-project-is-within-limits_1364960, Accessed on November 20, 2010.
6. Briscoe, John "War and Peace on the Indus?" *The News International*, April 5, 2010.
7. *The Dawn* "Water Dispute fuels India-Pakistan tensions" April 30, 2010.
8. Alam, Undala Z. "Questioning the Water Wars Rationale: A case study of the Indus Water Treaty" *The Geographical Journal* 164(4): 341-353, December 2002.
9. *The Indian Express* "Pakistan mismanaging Indus water- Qureshi" May 1, 2010.
10. Iyer, R "Pakistan's Questionable Move on Water" *Economic and Political Weekly*, 45(13): 10-12, March 27, 2010.
11. Kugelman, Michael & Hathaway, Robert M. (Ed.) "*Running on Empty: Pakistan's Water Crisis*" Woodrow Wilson International Center for Scholars, Asia Program, Washington D.C, 2009.
12. Kugleman, Michael, 2009, Pakistan's Water Crisis; Woodrow Wilson International Centre for Scholars in Washington, DC.
13. John, Wilson, "Water Security in South Asia: Issues and Policy Recommendations" ORF Issue Brief, Issue Brief #26, February 2011; p. 4.
14. "*Pakistan in the 21ˢᵗ Century: Vision 2030*" Executive Summary, Planning Commission, Government of Pakistan ,Available online at http://www. planningcommission.gov.pk/vision2030/Pak21stcentury/Chapter%20 Wise/07-Executive%20Summary.pdf, Accessed on November 20, 2010.
15. Anderson, Gretchen Cook "*NASA Satellites Unlock Secret to Northern India's Vanishing Water*" Available online at http://www.nasa.gov/topics/earth/features/ india_water.html, August 12, 2009 (Downloaded on November 20, 2010).

16. John, Wilson, "Water Security in South Asia: Issues and Policy Recommendations" ORF Issue Brief, Issue Brief #26, February 2011, pp. 3-4.

17. *The Financial Express* "Montek plans to put a price tag on water to minimise wastage" November 15, 2010.

18. John, Wilson, "Water Security in South Asia: Issues and Policy Recommendations" ORF Issue Brief, Issue Brief #26, February 2011; p. 5.

19. John, Wilson, "Water Security in South Asia: Issues and Policy Recommendations" ORF Issue Brief, Issue Brief #26, February 2011; p. 5.

20. World Bank *"Shared Views on Development and Climate Change"* International Bank for Reconstruction and Development/World Bank, Washington D.C., 2009.

21. John, Wilson: "Water Security in South Asia: Issues and Policy Recommendations" ORF Issue Brief, Issue Brief #26, February 2011; p. 6.

22. John, Wilson: "Water Security in South Asia: Issues and Policy Recommendations" ORF Issue Brief, Issue Brief #26, February 2011; p. 6.

23. Deacon, D., Pickering, M., Golding, P., & Murdock, G. *"A Practical Guide to Methods in Media and Cultural Analysis"*. London: Arnold. 1999, p. 117.

24. Stone, P. J., Dunphy, D. C., Smith, M. S., & Ogilvie, D. M. *"The General Inquirer: A computer approach to content analysis"*. Cambridge: MIT Press, 1966. p. 5.

25. Weber, R.P. *"Basic Content Analysis"*. London: Sage Publications, 1990, p. 5.

26. Krippendorff, K. "Content *Analysis: An Introduction to its Methodology"* London: Sage Publications. 2004, p. 18.

27. Hansen, A., Cottle, S., Negrine, R. & Newbold, C. *"Mass communication research methods"*. London: Macmillan. 1998, p. 92.

28. Neuendorf, K. *"The Content Analysis Guidebook"*. Thousand Oaks, CA: Sage Publications, 2002, p. 9.

29. World Bank *"Shared Views on Development and Climate Change"* International Bank for Reconstruction and Development/World Bank, Washington D.C 2009; p. 1.

30. World Bank *"Shared Views on Development and Climate Change"* International Bank for Reconstruction and Development/World Bank, Washington D.C., 2009; p. 10.

31. Deacon, D., Pickering, M., Golding, P., & Murdock, G. *"A Practical Guide to Methods in Media and Cultural Analysis"*. London: Arnold. 1999, p. 117.

32. Neuendorf, K: Neuendorf, K. *"The Content Analysis Guidebook"*. Thousand Oaks, CA: Sage Publications, 2002, pp. 5-7.

33. Neuendorf, K, Neuendorf, K. *"The Content Analysis Guidebook"*. Thousand Oaks, CA: Sage Publications, 2002, p. 41.

34. Shoemaker, P. & Reese, S. "Mediating the Message: Theories of influences on mass media content". White Plains, NY: Longman, 1996.

35. World Bank *"Shared Views on Development and Climate Change"* International

Bank for Reconstruction and Development/World Bank, Washington D.C., 2009; pp. 31-32.

36. Potter, W. & Levine-Donnerstein, D. "Rethinking validity and reliability in content analysis". *Journal of Applied Communication Research*, 27, 1999, pp. 258-284.

37. Deacon et all, 1999, "*A Practical Guide to Methods in Media and Cultural Analysis*". London: Arnold. 1999, p. 122.

38. Smith, Ronald D. "*Strategic planning for public relations*" Routledge, 2004, p. 296.

39. Krippendorff, K, "Content *Analysis: An Introduction to its Methodology*" London: Sage Publications. 2004, p. 23.

40. The value corresponds to the percentage of the articles that assign blame on the IWT within the subset of the total number (18%) of articles which mention IWT in the winter month. This pattern presenting shares is used consistently throughout the report.

41. The value corresponds to the percentage of articles that find Pakistan's assertions unreasonable, within the subset of the total number (28%) articles which mention this topic. This pattern of presenting shares is used consistently throughout the report.

42. The value corresponds to the percentage of the articles that agrees with the direct linkage of climate change to water shortage, within the subset of the total number (28%) of articles which mention this topic. This pattern of presenting shares is used consistently throughout the report.

Annexures

MCA: Primary Data

Pakistan Winter

	01	02	03	04	05
Article No.					
News Paper	The Dawn	The Daily Times	The Dawn	Pakistan Daily	The Dawn
Author	Aziz Malik	-	-	Sultan M Hali	Khaleeq Kiani
Length	557	283	158	996	511
Type of Article	News	News	News	Editorial	News
Date	January 04, 2010	January 08, 2010	January 11, 2010	January 15, 2010	January 16, 2010
POLITICAL DISCOURSE					
1 Has the IWT been put forward as the reason for water shortage/challenge?	4	3	4	1	4
2 Has Indian action and/or transgression been presented as a reason for water shortage/challenge?	4	3	1	1	4
3 Has political pressure against India been presented as a solution to water shortage?	4	4	1	1	4
4 Has water shortage lead to negative sentiments towards India?	4	4	1	1	4
5 Has increased cooperation between Pakistan and India been presented as a soultion to water issues?	4	1	3	3	4
6 Has water shortage led to conflict between stakeholders (People, institutions, political parties)?	3	3	4	4	4
7 Has inter-provincial water distribution/unfair implementation of domestic water sharing accord been argued to be the cause of water shortage?	3	4	4	4	4
8 Has implementation of domestic water sharing arrangements in letter and spirit been presented as a solution?	1	4	4	4	4

	01	02	03	04	05
Article No.					
News Paper	The Dawn	The Daily Times	The Dawn	Pakistan Daily	The Dawn
Author	Aziz Malik	-	-	Sultan M Hali	Khaleeq Kiani
Length	557	283	158	996	511
Type of Article	News	News	News	Editorial	News
Date	January 04, 2010	January 08, 2010	January 11, 2010	January 15, 2010	January 16, 2010
GOVERNANCE					
9 Have administrative lapses or challenges at the local, regional or national level been argued to be the cause of water shortage?	1	4	1	3	4
10 Should public water management be improved to solve water shortage?	1	4	4	3	4
11 Has insufficient water provision and storage infrastructure been argued to be the cause of water shortage?	1	4	4	1	4
12 Would investment/attention/technology solutions to water provision and storage infrastructure decrease water shortage?	1	4	4	1	4
PEOPLE, PRACTICE AND ENVIRONMENT					
13 Have changing climate/rainfall conditions caused water shortage?	4	4	4	1	1
14 Has water shortage led to environmental degradation?	4	4	4	4	4
15 Has underground water been affected?	4	4	4	4	4
16 Has the agricultural/agro dependent rural sector suffered due to water shortage?	1	4	1	1	1
17 Has water shortage affected domestic consumption?	3	4	4	4	4
18 Is crop diversification, or changing cropping patterns a solution to water shortage?	4	4	4	4	4
19 Is training/awareness mentioned as a solution to improve water efficiency ?	4	4	4	1	4
1: Yes					
2: No					
3: Ambiguous: weak assertions or difficult to comprehend					
4: Not Mentioned: Query not applicable or not referred					
** This is the unedited questionnaire that the main text draws on					

Article No.		06	07	08	09	10
News Paper		The Pak Tribune	The Daily Times	The Dawn	The Daily Times	The Dawn
Author		-	Mahtab Bashir	Khaleeq Kiani	-	M.B. Kalhoro
Length		300	399	555	637	448
Type of Article		Comment	News	Feature	News	News
Date		January 22, 2010	January 23, 2010	January 25, 2010	January 29, 2010	February 01, 2010
POLITICAL DISCOURSE						
1	Has the IWT been put forth as the reason for water shortage/challenge?	4	4	4	4	4
2	Has Indian action and/or transgression been presented as a reason for water shortage/challenge?	1	4	4	4	4
3	Has political pressure against India been presented as a solution to water shortage?	1	4	4	4	4
4	Has water shortage led to negative sentiments towards India?	1	4	4	4	4
5	Has the increased cooperation between Pakistan and India been presented as a solution to water issues?	3	4	4	4	4
6	Has water shortage led to conflict between stakeholders (People, institutions, political parties)?	1	4	4	1	3
7	Has inter-provincial water distribution/unfair implementation of domestic water sharing accord been argued to be the cause of water shortage?	4	4	4	1	4
8	Has implementation of domestic water sharing arrangements in letter and spirit been presented as a solution?	4	4	4	4	4

Article No.	06	07	08	09	10
News Paper	The Pak Tribune	The Daily Times	The Dawn	The Daily Times	The Dawn
Author	-	Mahtab Bashir	Khaleeq Kiani	-	M.B. Kalhoro
Length	300	399	555	637	448
Type of Article	Comment	News	Feature	News	News
Date	January 22, 2010	January 23, 2010	January 25, 2010	January 29, 2010	February 01, 2010
GOVERNANCE					
9 Have administrative lapses or challenges at the local, regional or national level been argued to be the cause of water shortage?	4	1	4	4	1
10 Should public water management be improved to solve water shortage?	4	1	1	4	1
11 Has insufficient water provision and storage infrastructure been argued to be the cause of water shortage?	4	4	4	4	1
12 Will investment/attention/technology solutions to water provision and storage infrastructure decrease water shortage?	4	4	4	4	4
PEOPLE, PRACTICE AND ENVIRONMENT					
13 Have changing climate/rainfall conditions caused water shortage?		4	1	4	1
14 Has water shortage led to environmental degradation?	4	4	4	4	4
15 Has undergound water been affected?	4	4	4	4	4
16 Has the agricultural/agro dependent rural sector suffered due to water shortage?	1	4	1	1	1
17 Has water shortage affected domestic consumption?	4	1	4	1	4
18 Is crop diversification, or changing cropping patterns a solution to water shortage?	4	4	4	4	4
19 Is training/awareness mentioned as a solution to improve water efficiency ?	4	4	4	4	4
1: Yes					
2: No					
3: Ambiguous: weak assertions or difficult to comprehend					
4: Not Mentioned: Query not applicable or not referred					
** This is the unedited questionnaire that the main text draws on					

Article No.	11	12	13	14	15
News Paper	The Dawn	The Dawn	The Pak Tribune	The Nation	The Dawn
Author	-	-	-	-	Kalbe Ali
Length	138	115	452	562	395
Type of Article	News	News	News	Comment	News
Date	February 02, 2010	February 03, 2010	February 03, 2010	February 06, 2010	February 07, 2010
POLITICAL DISCOURSE					
1 Has the IWT been put forth as the reason for water shortage/challenge?	3	4	4	1	4
2 Has Indian action and/or transgression been presented as a reason for water shortage/challenge?	3	1	4	1	4
3 Has political pressure against India been presented as a solution to water shortage?	3	3	4	1	4
4 Has water shortage led to negative sentiments towards India?	4	4	4	1	4
5 Has increased cooperation between Pakistan and India been presented as a solution to water issues?	1	3	4	3	4
6 Has water shortage lead to conflict between stakeholders (People, institutions, political parties)?	4	4	1	4	4
7 Has inter-provincial water distribution/unfair implementation of domestic water sharing accord been argued to be the cause of water shortage?	4	4	1	4	1
8 Has implementation of domestic water sharing arrangements in letter and spirit been presented as a solution?	4	4	1	4	1

Article No.	11	12	13	14	15
News Paper	The Dawn	The Dawn	The Pak Tribune	The Nation	The Dawn
Author	-	-	-	-	Kalbe Ali
Length	138	115	452	562	395
Type of Article	News	News	News	Comment	News
Date	February 02, 2010	February 03, 2010	February 03, 2010	February 06, 2010	February 07, 2010
GOVERNANCE					
9 Have administrative lapses or challenges at the local, regional or national level been argued to be the cause of water shortage?	4	4	4	4	4
10 Should public water management be improved to solve water shortage?	4	4	4	4	4
11 Has insufficient water provision and storage infrastructure been argued to be the cause of water shortage?	4	4	4	4	4
12 Will investment/attention/technology solutions to water provision and storage infrastructure decrease water shortage?	4	4	4	1	4
PEOPLE, PRACTICE AND ENVIRONMENT					
13 Have changing climate/rainfall conditions caused water shortage?	4	4	4	4	1
14 Has water shortage led to environmental degradation?	4	4	4	4	4
15 Has undergound water been affected?	4	4	4	4	4
16 Has the agricultural/agro dependent rural sector suffered due to water shortage?	4	4	4	1	4
17 Has water shortage affected domestic consumption?	4	4	4	1	4
18 Is crop diversification, or changing cropping patterns a solution to water shortage?	4	4	4	4	4
19 Is training/awareness mentioned as a solution to improve water efficiency ?	4	4	4	4	4

1: Yes
2: No
3: Ambiguous: weak assertions or difficult to comprehend
4: Not Mentioned: Query not applicable or not referred

** This is the unedited questionnaire that the main text draws on

Article No.	16	17	18	19	20
News Paper	The Daily Times	The Pak Tribune	The Dawn	The Dawn	The Dawn
Author	-	-	Ahmad Fraz Khan	Saleem Shaikh	Ashfak Bokhari
Length	277	596	421	884	1175
Type of Article	News	News	News	Feature	Feature
Date	February 08, 2010	February 10, 2010	February 11, 2010	February 15, 2010	February 15, 2010
POLITICAL DISCOURSE					
1 Has the IWT been put forth as the reason for water shortage/challenge?	4	4	3	4	4
2 Has Indian action and/or transgression been presented as a reason for water shortage/challenge?	1	4	3	4	1
3 Has political pressure against India been presented as a solution to water shortage?	1	4	2	4	1
4 Has water shortage led to negative sentiments towards India?	4	4	4	4	1
5 Has increased cooperation between Pakistan and India been presented as a solution to water issues?	3	4	1	4	3
6 Has water shortage led to conflict between stakeholders (People, institutions, political parties)?	4	1	4	4	1
7 Has inter-provincial water distribution/unfair implementation of domestic water sharing accord been argued to be the cause of water shortage?	4	1	4	4	1
8 Has implementation of domestic water sharing arrangements in letter and spirit been presented as a solution?	4	1	4	4	1

Article No.	16	17	18	19	20
News Paper	The Daily Times	The Pak Tribune	The Dawn	The Dawn	The Dawn
Author	-	-	Ahmad Fraz Khan	Saleem Shaikh	Ashfak Bokhari
Length	277	596	421	884	1175
Type of Article	News	News	News	Feature	Feature
Date	February 08, 2010	February 10, 2010	February 11, 2010	February 15, 2010	February 15, 2010
GOVERNANCE					
9 Have administrative lapses or challenges at the local, regional or national level been argued to be the cause of water shortage?	1	3	4	1	1
10 Should public water management be improved to solve water shortage?	4	3	4	1	4
11 Has insufficient water provision and storage infrastructure been argued to be the cause of water shortage?	4	4	4	1	4
12 Will investment/attention/technology solutions to water provision and storage infrastructure decrease water shortage?	4	4	4	1	4
PEOPLE, PRACTICE AND ENVIRONMENT					
13 Have changing climate/rainfall conditions caused water shortage?	4	4	1	1	1
14 Has water shortage led to environmental degradation?	4	1	4	4	4
15 Has undergound water been affected?	4	4	4	4	4
16 Has the agricultural/agro dependent rural sector suffered due to water shortage?	4	1	4	1	1
17 Has water shortage affected domestic consumption?	4	1	4	4	4
18 Is crop diversification, or changing cropping patterns a solution to water shortage?	4	4	4	4	4
19 Is training/awareness mentioned as a solution to improve water efficiency ?	4	4	4	4	4

1: Yes
2: No
3: Ambiguous: weak assertions or difficult to comprehend
4: Not Mentioned: Query not applicable or not referred

** This is the unedited questionnaire that the main text draws on

Article No.	21	22	23	24	25
News Paper	The Nation	The Dawn	The Dawn	The Dawn	The Daily Times
Author	-	-	-	Ahmer Bilal Soofi	-
Length	657	161	154	916	133
Type of Article	News	News	News	Comment	News
Date	February 17, 2010	February 19, 2010	February 19, 2010	February 20, 2010	February 20, 2010

POLITICAL DISCOURSE

		21	22	23	24	25
1	Has the IWT been put forth as the reason for water shortage/challenge?	1	4	4	3	4
2	Has Indian action and/or transgression been presented as a reason for water shortage/challenge?	1	1	4	3	4
3	Has political pressure against India been presented as a solution to water shortage?	3	4	4	2	4
4	Has water shortage led to negative sentiments towards India?	1	3	4	4	4
5	Has increased cooperation between Pakistan and India been presented as a solution to water issues?	1	4	4	1	1
6	Has water shortage led to conflict between stakeholders (People, institutions, political parties)?	1	4	1	4	4
7	Has inter-provincial water distribution/unfair implementation of domestic water sharing accord been argued to be the cause of water shortage?	1	4	1	4	4
8	Has implementation of domestic water sharing arrangements in letter and spirit been presented as a solution?	1	4	1	4	4

Article No.	16	17	18	19	20
News Paper	The Daily Times	The Pak Tribune	The Dawn	The Dawn	The Dawn
Author	-	-	Ahmad Fraz Khan	Saleem Shaikh	Ashfak Bokhari
Length	277	596	421	884	1175
Type of Article	News	News	News	Feature	Feature
Date	February 08, 2010	February 10, 2010	February 11, 2010	February 15, 2010	February 15, 2010
GOVERNANCE					
9 Have administrative lapses or challenges at the local, regional or national level been argued to be the cause of water shortage?	3	1	4	4	4
10 Should public water management be improved to solve water shortage?	3	4	4	4	4
11 Has insufficient water provision and storage infrastructure been argued to be the cause of water shortage?	4	4	4	4	4
12 Will investment/attention/technology solutions to water provision and storage infrastructure decrease water shortage?	4	4	4	4	4
PEOPLE, PRACTICE AND ENVIRONMENT					
13 Have changing climate/rainfall conditions caused water shortage?	1	4	4	3	4
14 Has water shortage led to environmental degradation?	4	4	4	4	4
15 Has underground water been affected?	4	4	4	4	4
16 Has the agricultural/agro dependent rural sector suffered due to water shortage?	1	4	4	4	4
17 Has water shortage affected domestic consumption?	4	4	4	4	4
18 Is crop diversification, or changing cropping patterns a solution to water shortage?	4	4	4	4	4
19 Is training/awareness mentioned as a solution to improve water efficiency ?	4	4	4	4	4

1: Yes
2: No
3: Ambiguous: weak assertions or difficult to comprehend
4: Not Mentioned: Query not applicable or not referred

** This is the unedited questionnaire that the main text draws on

Article No.	26	27	28	29	30
News Paper	The Dawn	The Daily Times	The Pak Tribune	The Dawn	The Nation
Author	Qamaruddin	Mohammad Ali Talpur	-	Mohammad Hussain Khan	-
Length	394	1261	332	565	312
Type of Article	News	Comment	News	News	News
Date	February 21, 2010	February 21, 2010	February 21, 2010	February 23, 2010	February 23, 2010

POLITICAL DISCOURSE

		26	27	28	29	30
1	Has the IWT been put forth as the reason for water shortage/ challenge?	4	4	4	4	4
2	Has Indian action and/or transgression been presented as a reason for water shortage/challenge?	4	4	4	4	4
3	Has political pressure against India been presented as a solution to water shortage?	4	4	4	4	4
4	Has water shortage led to negative sentiments towards India?	4	4	4	4	4
5	Has increased cooperation between Pakistan and India been presented as a solution to water issues?	4	4	4	4	4
6	Has water shortage lead to conflict between stakeholders (People, institutions, political parties)?	1	1	3	4	4
7	Has inter-provincial water distribution/unfair implementation of domestic water sharing accord been argued to be the cause of water shortage?	4	1	1	1	3
8	Has implementation of domestic water sharing arrangements in letter and spirit been presented as a solution?	4	1	1	1	1

Article No.	26	27	28	29	30
News Paper	The Dawn	The Daily Times	The Pak Tribune	The Dawn	The Nation
Author	Qamaruddin	Mohammad Ali Talpur	-	Mohammad Hussain Khan	-
Length	394	1261	332	565	312
Type of Article	News	Comment	News	News	News
Date	February 21, 2010	February 21, 2010	February 21, 2010	February 23, 2010	February 23, 2010
GOVERNANCE					
9 Have administrative lapses or challenges at the local, regional or national level been argued to be the cause of water shortage?	1	1	4	4	4
10 Should public water management be improved to solve water shortage?	1	3	4	4	4
11 Has insufficient water provision and storage infrastructure been argued to be the cause of water shortage?	1	1	4	4	4
12 Will investment/attention/technology solutions to water provision and storage infrastructure decrease water shortage?	4	4	4	4	4
PEOPLE, PRACTICE AND ENVIRONMENT					
13 Have changing climate/rainfall conditions caused water shortage?	4	4	4	4	4
14 Has water shortage led to environmental degradation?	4	1	4	4	4
15 Has underground water been affected?	4	4	4	4	4
16 Has the agricultural/agro dependent rural sector suffered due to water shortage?	1	1	1	4	4
17 Has water shortage affected domestic consumption?	1	1	4	4	4
18 Is crop diversification, or changing cropping patterns a solution to water shortage?	4	4	4	4	4
19 Is training/awareness mentioned as a solution to improve water efficiency ?	4	4	4	4	4

1: Yes
2: No
3: Ambiguous: weak assertions or difficult to comprehend
4: Not Mentioned: Query not applicable or not referred

** This is the unedited questionnaire that the main text draws on

Article No.	31	32	33	34	35
News Paper	The Pak Tribune	The Dawn	The Nation	The Daily Times	The Pak Tribune
Author	-	Kalbe Ali	Khalid Iqbal	-	Zaheerul Hassan
Length	388	364	778	439	1364
Type of Article	News	News	Comment	News	Comment
Date	February 23, 2010	February 27, 2010	March 01, 2010	March 02, 2010	March 03, 2010
POLITICAL DISCOURSE					
1 Has the IWT been put forth as the reason for water shortage/challenge?	4	4	4	4	4
2 Has Indian action and/or transgression been presented as a reason for water shortage/challenge?	4	4	1	3	1
3 Has political pressure against India been presented as a solution to water shortage?	4	4	4	3	1
4 Has water shortage led to negative sentiments towards India?	4	4	4	3	1
5 Has increased cooperation between Pakistan and India been presented as a solution to water issues?	4	4	1	1	3
6 Has water shortage lead to conflict between stakeholders (People, institutions, political parties)?	4	4	4	4	4
7 Has inter-provincial water distribution/unfair implementation of domestic water sharing accord been argued to be the cause of water shortage?	3	4	4	1	4
8 Has implementation of domestic water sharing arrangements in letter and spirit been presented as a solution?	1	4	4	1	4

Article No.	31	32	33	34	35
News Paper	The Pak Tribune	The Dawn	The Nation	The Daily Times	The Pak Tribune
Author	-	Kalbe Ali	Khalid Iqbal	-	Zaheerul Hassan
Length	388	364	778	439	1364
Type of Article	News	News	Comment	News	Comment
Date	February 23, 2010	February 27, 2010	March 01, 2010	March 02, 2010	March 03, 2010
GOVERNANCE					
9 Have administrative lapses or challenges at the local, regional or national level been argued to be the cause of water shortage?	4	4	4	1	4
10 Should public water management be improved to solve water shortage?	4	4	4	4	4
11 Has insufficient water provision and storage infrastructure been argued to be the cause of water shortage?	4	4	4	4	4
12 Will investment/attention/technology solutions to water provision and storage infrastructure decrease water shortage?	4	1	4	4	4
PEOPLE, PRACTICE AND ENVIRONMENT					
13 Have changing climate/rainfall conditions caused water shortage?	4	1	4	4	4
14 Has water shortage led to environmental degradation?	4	4	4	4	4
15 Has underground water been affected?	4	4	4	4	4
16 Has the agricultural/agro dependent rural sector suffered due to water shortage?	4	1	4	1	1
17 Has water shortage affected domestic consumption?	4	4	4	1	4
18 Is crop diversification, or changing cropping patterns a solution to water shortage?	4	4	4	4	4
19 Is training/awareness mentioned as a solution to improve water efficiency ?	4	4	4	4	4
1: Yes					
2: No					
3: Ambiguous: weak assertions or difficult to comprehend					
4: Not Mentioned: Query not applicable or not referred					
** This is the unedited questionnaire that the main text draws on					

	36	37	38	39	40
Article No.					
News Paper	The Pakistan Observer	The Dawn	The Dawn	The Daily Times	The Daily Times
Author	Gauhar Zahid Malik	Ahmad Hayat	Qurban Ali Khushik	Ijaz Kakakhel	-
Length	1415	968	721	728	133
Type of Article	Comment	Editorial	Feature	News	News
Date	March 03, 2010	March 09, 2010	March 10, 2010	March 17, 2010	March 17, 2010

POLITICAL DISCOURSE

		36	37	38	39	40
1	Has the IWT been put forth as the reason for water shortage/challenge?	4	4	4	4	4
2	Has Indian action and/or transgression been presented as a reason for water shortage/challenge?	1	4		4	4
3	Has political pressure against India been presented as a solution to water shortage?	3	4	4	4	4
4	Has water shortage led to negative sentiments towards India?	1	4	4	4	4
5	Has increased cooperation between Pakistan and India been presented as a soultion to water issues?	3	4	4	4	4
6	Has water shortage led to conflict between stakeholders (People, institutions, political parties)?	4	4	4	4	4
7	Has inter-provincial water distribution/unfair implementation of domestic water sharing accord been argued to be the cause of water shortage?	4	4	4	4	4
8	Has implementation of domestic water sharing arrangements in letter and spirit been presented as a solution?	4	4	4	4	4

Article No.	36	37	38	39	40
News Paper	The Pakistan Observer	The Dawn	The Dawn	The Daily Times	The Daily Times
Author	Gauhar Zahid Malik	Ahmad Hayat	Qurban Ali Khushik	Ijaz Kakakhel	-
Length	1415	968	721	728	133
Type of Article	Comment	Editorial	Feature	News	News
Date	March 03, 2010	March 09, 2010	March 10, 2010	March 17, 2010	March 17, 2010
GOVERNANCE					
9 Have administrative lapses or challenges at the local, regional or national level been argued to be the cause of water shortage?	4	1	4	4	1
10 Should public water management be improved to solve water shortage?	4	1	4	4	1
11 Has insufficient water provision and storage infrastructure been argued to be the cause of water shortage?	4	1	4	4	4
12 Will investment/attention/technology solutions to water provision and storage infrastructure decrease water shortage?	4	1	1	4	1
PEOPLE, PRACTICE AND ENVIRONMENT					
13 Have changing climate/rainfall conditions caused water shortage?	4	1	1	1	4
14 Has water shortage led to environmental degradation?	4	4	4	4	4
15 Has undergound water been affected?	4	1	1	4	4
16 Has the agricultural/agro dependent rural sector suffered due to water shortage?	1	1	1	1	1
17 Has water shortage affected domestic consumption?	4	1	1	4	4
18 Is crop diversification, or changing cropping patterns a solution to water shortage?	4	4	4	1	4
19 Is training/awareness mentioned as a solution to improve water efficiency ?	4	1	4	1	1

1: Yes
2: No
3: Ambiguous: weak assertions or difficult to comprehend
4: Not Mentioned: Query not applicable or not referred

** This is the unedited questionnaire that the main text draws on

Article No.	41	42	43	44	45
News Paper	The Dawn	The Dawn	The Nation	The Daily Times	The Nation
Author	-	-	M. Zahur-ul-Haq	-	-
Length	303	538	853	512	245
Type of Article	News	News	Comment	News	News
Date	March 19, 2010	March 23, 2010	March 23, 2010	March 26, 2010	March 27, 2010
POLITICAL DISCOURSE					
1 Has the IWT been put forth as the reason for water shortage/challenge?	1	1	4	4	4
2 Has Indian action and/or transgression been presented as a reason for water shortage/challenge?	1	1	1	1	1
3 Has political pressure against India been presented as a solution to water shortage?	3	3	1	4	3
4 Has water shortage led to negative sentiments towards India?	3	1	1	3	3
5 Has increased cooperation between Pakistan and India been presented as a solution to water issues?	3	3	2	4	1
6 Has water shortage lead to conflict between stakeholders (People, institutions, political parties)?	3	1	4	4	4
7 Has inter-provincial water distribution/unfair implementation of domestic water sharing accord been argued to be the cause of water shortage?	1	1	4	4	4
8 Has implementation of domestic water sharing arrangements in letter and spirit been presented as a solution?	1	1	4	4	4

Article No.	41	42	43	44	45
News Paper	The Dawn	The Dawn	The Nation	The Daily Times	The Nation
Author	-	-	M. Zahur-ul-Haq	-	-
Length	303	538	853	512	245
Type of Article	News	News	Comment	News	News
Date	March 19, 2010	March 23, 2010	March 23, 2010	March 26, 2010	March 27, 2010
GOVERNANCE					
9 Have administrative lapses or challenges at the local, regional or national level been argued to be the cause of water shortage?	4	1	1	1	1
10 Should public water management be improved to solve water shortage?	1	4	4	1	4
11 Has insufficient water provision and storage infrastructure been argued to be the cause of water shortage?	1	4	4	1	4
12 Will investment/attention/technology solutions to water provision and storage infrastructure decrease water shortage?	1	4	4	4	4
PEOPLE, PRACTICE AND ENVIRONMENT					
13 Have changing climate/rainfall conditions caused water shortage?	4	4	1	4	4
14 Has water shortage led to environmental degradation?	4	4	4	4	4
15 Has undergound water been affected?	4	4	1	4	4
16 Has the agricultural/agro dependent rural sector suffered due to water shortage?	1	1	1	1	1
17 Has water shortage affected domestic consumption?	4	1	4	1	4
18 Is crop diversification, or changing cropping patterns a solution to water shortage?	4	4	4	4	4
19 Is training/awareness mentioned as a solution to improve water efficiency ?	1	4	4	4	4

1: Yes
2: No
3: Ambiguous: weak assertions or difficult to comprehend
4: Not Mentioned: Query not applicable or not referred

** This is the unedited questionnaire that the main text draws on

Article No.	46	47	48	49	50
News Paper	The Daily Times	The Daily Times	The Dawn	The Daily Times	The Nation
Author	Zeeshan Javaid	-	-	Iftikhar Gilani	-
Length	552	218	290	388	487
Type of Article	News	News	News	News	Comment
Date	March 28, 2010	March 28, 2010	March 29, 2010	March 29, 2010	March 29, 2010

POLITICAL DISCOURSE

1 Has the IWT been put forth as the reason for water shortage/challenge?	4	4	4	4	4
2 Has Indian action and/or transgression been presented as a reason for water shortage/challenge?	4	3	3	2	1
3 Has political pressure against India been presented as a solution to water shortage?	4	4	4	4	1
4 Has water shortage led to negative sentiments towards India?	4	4	4	4	3
5 Has increased cooperation between Pakistan and India been presented as a solution to water issues?	4	1	1	4	4
6 Has water shortage lead to conflict between stakeholders (People, institutions, political parties)?	4	4	4	4	4
7 Has inter-provincial water distribution/unfair implementation of domestic water sharing accord been argued to be the cause of water shortage?	4	4	4	4	4
8 Has implementation of domestic water sharing arrangements in letter and spirit been presented as a solution?	4	4	4	4	4

Article No.	46	47	48	49	50
News Paper	The Daily Times	The Daily Times	The Dawn	The Daily Times	The Nation
Author	Zeeshan Javaid	-	-	Iftikhar Gilani	-
Length	552	218	290	388	487
Type of Article	News	News	News	News	Comment
Date	March 28, 2010	March 28, 2010	March 29, 2010	March 29, 2010	March 29, 2010
GOVERNANCE					
9 Have administrative lapses or challenges at the local, regional or national level been argued to be the cause of water shortage?	4	4	4	1	1
10 Should public water management be improved to solve water shortage?	4	4	4	1	4
11 Has insufficient water provision and storage infrastructure been argued to be the cause of water shortage?	4	4	4	1	4
12 Will investment/attention/technology solutions to water provision and storage infrastructure decrease water shortage?	4	4	4	4	4
PEOPLE, PRACTICE AND ENVIRONMENT					
13 Have changing climate/rainfall conditions caused water shortage?	1	4	4	4	4
14 Has water shortage led to environmental degradation?	4	4	4	4	4
15 Has undergound water been affected?	4	4	4	4	4
16 Has the agricultural/agro dependent rural sector suffered due to water shortage?	4	4	4	4	4
17 Has water shortage affected domestic consumption?	4	4	4	4	1
18 Is crop diversification, or changing cropping patterns a solution to water shortage?	4	4	4	4	4
19 Is training/awareness mentioned as a solution to improve water efficiency ?	4	4	4	4	4

1: Yes
2: No
3: Ambiguous: weak assertions or difficult to comprehend
4: Not Mentioned: Query not applicable or not referred

** This is the unedited questionnaire that the main text draws on

India Winter

		01	02	03	04	05
Article No.		The Tribune	The Tribune	The Indian Express	The Hindustan Times	The Indian Express
News Paper		Naveen S Garewal	-	-	Praveen Donthi	-
Author		537	409	303	1202	412
Length		News	News	News	Feature	News
Type of Article		January 01, 2010	January 07, 2010	January 09, 2010	January 16, 2010	January 22, 2010
Date						
POLITICAL DISCOURSE						
1	Are unfair/flawed provisions of IWT the reasons for water shortage?	4	4	4	4	4
2	Has regional water shortage led Pakistan to accuse India of breaching water agreements?	4	4	4	4	4
3	Have Pakistan's assertions of India not abiding by the water agreements suggested as being unreasonable?	4	4	4	4	4
4	Should Pakistan and India intensify cooperation to resolve water issues?	4	4	4	4	4
5	Has uneven inter-provincial water distribution/usage been argued to be the cause of water shortage/issue?	4	4	4	4	4
6	Has water shortage led to conflict/disagreement between stakeholders (People, Institutions, Political Parties)?	4	3	4	4	4
7	Has water been employed as a socio-political tool by extremist elements?	4	4	4	4	4
GOVERNANCE						
8	Have administrative lapses or challenges at the local, regional or national level been argued to be the cause of water shortage/issue?	4	4	3	1	1
9	Should public water management/Regulation be improved to solve water shortage?	4	4	3	3	1
10	Has insufficient water/supply provision and storage infrastructure been argued to be the cause of water shortage/issue?	4	4	3	4	4

Article No.	01	02	03	04	05
News Paper	The Tribune	The Tribune	The Indian Express	The Hindustan Times	The Indian Express
Author	Naveen S Garewal	-	-	Praveen Donthi	-
Length	537	409	303	1202	412
Type of Article	News	News	News	Feature	News
Date	January 01, 2010	January 07, 2010	January 09, 2010	January 16, 2010	January 22, 2010
11 Will investment in water provision/technology provision and storage infrastructure decrease water shortage?	4	4	1	4	4
12 Has public-private partnership/better water pricing partnership been suggested to improve water provision?	4	4	4	4	4
PEOPLE, PRACTICE AND ENVIRONMENT					
13 Have changing climate/rainfall conditions caused water shortage?	4	4	4	4	4
14 Has water shortage led to environmental degradation/issues?	1	4	4	3	4
15 Has undergound water been affected?	1	4	4	4	4
16 Has the agricultural/agro dependent rural sector suffered due to water shortage?	4	4	1	1	4
17 Has water shortage affected domestic consumption?	4	4	4	4	4
18 Is crop diversification, or changing cropping patterns a solution to water shortage?	4	4	4	4	4
19 Is training/awareness mentioned as a solution to improve water efficiency ?	4	4	3	4	4
1: Yes					
2: No					
3: Ambiguous: weak assertions or difficult to comprehend					
4: Not Mentioned: Query not applicable or not referred					
** This is the unedited questionnaire that the main text draws on					

Article No.	06	07	08	09	10
News Paper	The Telegraph	The Times of India	The Telegraph	The Hindustan Times	The Indian Express
Author	-	-	S.L. Rao	-	Geeta Gupta
Length	447	597	1256	437	372
Type of Article	News	Feature	Comment	News	News
Date	January 23, 2010	January 24, 2010	January 25, 2010	February 04, 2010	February 06, 2010
POLITICAL DISCOURSE					
1 Are unfair/flawed provisions of IWT the reasons for water shortage?	4	4	4	4	4
2 Has regional water shortage led Pakistan to accuse India of breaching water agreements?	3	4	4	4	4
3 Have Pakistan's assertions of India not abiding by the water agreements suggested as being unreasonable?	4	4	4	4	4
4 Should Pakistan and India intensify cooperation to resolve water issues?	1	4	4	4	4
5 Has uneven inter-provincial water distribution/usage been argued to be the cause of water shortage/issue?	4	4	4	4	4
6 Has water shortage led to conflict/disagreement between stakeholders (People, Institutions, Political Parties)?	4	1	4	4	4
7 Has water been employed as a socio-political tool by extremist elements?	4	4	4	4	4
GOVERNANCE					
8 Have administrative lapses or challenges at the local, regional or national level been argued to be the cause of water shortage/issue?	4	1	1	4	3
9 Should public water management/Regulation be improved to solve water shortage?	4	1	1	4	1
10 Has insufficient water/supply provision and storage infrastructure been argued to be the cause of water shortage/issue?	4	4	3	4	4

	06	07	08	09	10
Article No.					
News Paper	The Telegraph	The Times of India	The Telegraph	The Hindustan Times	The Indian Express
Author	-	-	S.L. Rao	-	Geeta Gupta
Length	447	597	1256	437	372
Type of Article	News	Feature	Comment	News	News
Date	January 23, 2010	January 24, 2010	January 25, 2010	February 04, 2010	February 06, 2010
11 Will investment in water provision/technology provision and storage infrastructure decrease water shortage?	4	4	3	4	4
12 Has public-private partnership/better water pricing partnership been suggested to improve water provision?	4	4	4	4	4
PEOPLE, PRACTICE AND ENVIRONMENT					
13 Have changing climate/rainfall conditions caused water shortage?	4	4	4	1	1
14 Has water shortage led to environmental degradation/issues?	4	4	4	4	4
15 Has undergound water been affected?	4	4	1	4	1
16 Has the agricultural/agro dependent rural sector suffered due to water shortage?	4	1	1	1	4
17 Has water shortage affected domestic consumption?	4	3	4	4	3
18 Is crop diversification, or changing cropping patterns a solution to water shortage?	4	4	4	4	4
19 Is training/awareness mentioned as a solution to improve water efficiency ?	4	4	4	4	4

1: Yes
2: No
3: Ambiguous: weak assertions or difficult to comprehend
4: Not Mentioned: Query not applicable or not referred

** This is the unedited questionnaire that the main text draws on

Article No.	11	12	13	14	15
News Paper	The Times of India	The Tribune	The Indian Express	The Tribune	The Hindu
Author	Prithvijit Mitra	-	Manoj Prasad	Vibha Sharma	Siddharth Vara-darajan
Length	456	205	544	527	518
Type of Article	News	News	Feature	News	News
Date	February 08, 2010	February 09, 2010	February 12, 2010	February 12, 2010	February 14, 2010
POLITICAL DISCOURSE					
1 Are unfair/flawed provisions of IWT the reasons for water shortage?	4	4	4	4	4
2 Has regional water shortage led Pakistan to accuse India of breaching water agreements?	4	4	4	4	1
3 Have Pakistan's assertions of India not abiding by the water agreements suggested as being unreasonable?	4	4	4	4	3
4 Should Pakistan and India intensify cooperation to resolve water issues?	4	4	4	4	4
5 Has uneven inter-provincial water distribution/usage been argued to be the cause of water shortage/issue?	4	4	4	1	4
6 Has water shortage led to conflict/disagreement between stakeholders (People, Institutions, Political Parties)?	4	4	4	4	4
7 Has water been employed as a socio-political tool by extremist elements?	4	4	4	4	1
GOVERNANCE					
8 Have administrative lapses or challenges at the local, regional or national level been argued to be the cause of water shortage/issue?	1	3	4	4	4
9 Should public water management/Regulation be improved to solve water shortage?	1	3	3	1	4
10 Has insufficient water/supply provision and storage infrastructure been argued to be the cause of water shortage/issue?	4	4	1	4	4

	11	12	13	14	15
Article No.	11	12	13	14	15
News Paper	The Times of India	The Tribune	The Indian Express	The Tribune	The Hindu
Author	Prithvijit Mitra	-	Manoj Prasad	Vibha Sharma	Siddharth Varadarajan
Length	456	205	544	527	518
Type of Article	News	News	Feature	News	News
Date	February 08, 2010	February 09, 2010	February 12, 2010	February 12, 2010	February 14, 2010
11 Will investment in water provision/technology provision and storage infrastructure decrease water shortage?	4	4	1	4	4
12 Has public-private partnership/better water pricing partnership been suggested to improve water provision?	4	4	4	4	4
PEOPLE, PRACTICE AND ENVIRONMENT					
13 Have changing climate/rainfall conditions caused water shortage?	4	4	1	4	4
14 Has water shortage led to environmental degradation/issues?	1	4	4	1	4
15 Has undergound water been affected?	1	1	4	1	4
16 Has the agricultural/agro dependent rural sector suffered due to water shortage?	4	4	1	1	4
17 Has water shortage affected domestic consumption?	4	4	3	4	4
18 Is crop diversification, or changing cropping patterns a solution to water shortage?	4	4	4	4	4
19 Is training/awareness mentioned as a solution to improve water efficiency ?	4	4	3	4	4
1: Yes					
2: No					
3: Ambiguous: weak assertions or difficult to comprehend					
4: Not Mentioned: Query not applicable or not referred					
** This is the unedited questionnaire that the main text draws on					

Article No.	16	17	18	19	20
News Paper	The Tribune	The Tribune	The Telegraph	The Indian Express	The Times of India
Author	Jangveer Singh	Sushil Manav	ARCHIS MOHAN	Girish Sharma	-
Length	291	330	457	181	633
Type of Article	News	News	News	News	News
Date	February 14, 2010	February 14, 2010	February 15, 2010	February 23, 2010	February 23, 2010
POLITICAL DISCOURSE					
1 Are unfair/flawed provisions of IWT the reasons for water shortage?	4	4	4	4	4
2 Has regional water shortage led Pakistan to accuse India of breaching water agreements?	4	4	4	4	1
3 Have Pakistan's assertions of India not abiding by the water agreements suggested as being unreasonable?	4	4	3	4	1
4 Should Pakistan and India intensify cooperation to resolve water issues?	4	4	4	4	4
5 Has uneven inter-provincial water distribution/usage been argued to be the cause of water shortage/issue?	4	4	4	4	4
6 Has water shortage led to conflict/disagreement between stakeholders (People, Institutions, Political Parties)?	4	4	4	4	1
7 Has water been employed as a socio-political tool by extremist elements?	4	4	1	4	1
GOVERNANCE					
8 Have administrative lapses or challenges at the local, regional or national level been argued to be the cause of water shortage/issue?	1	4	4	1	4
9 Should public water management/Regulaion be improved to solve water shortage?	3	4	4	4	4
10 Has insufficient water/supply provision and storage infrastructure been argued to be the cause of water shortage/issue?	1	1	4	1	4

Article No.	16	17	18	19	20
News Paper	The Tribune	The Tribune	The Telegraph	The Indian Express	The Times of India
Author	Jangveer Singh	Sushil Manav	ARCHIS MOHAN	Girish Sharma	-
Length	291	330	457	181	633
Type of Article	News	News	News	News	News
Date	February 14, 2010	February 14, 2010	February 15, 2010	February 23, 2010	February 23, 2010
11 Will investment in water provision/technology provision and storage infrastructure decrease water shortage?	1	1	4	4	4
12 Has public-private partnership/better water pricing partnership been suggested to improve water provision?	1	4	4	4	4
PEOPLE, PRACTICE AND ENVIRONMENT					
13 Have changing climate/rainfall conditions caused water shortage?	4	4	4	4	1
14 Has water shortage led to environmental degradation/issues?	4	4	4	4	4
15 Has undergound water been affected?	4	4	4	4	4
16 Has the agricultural/agro dependent rural sector suffered due to water shortage?	1	3	4	3	4
17 Has water shortage affected domestic consumption?	1	3	4	3	4
18 Is crop diversification, or changing cropping patterns a solution to water shortage?	4	4	4	4	4
19 Is training/awareness mentioned as a solution to improve water efficiency ?	4	4	4	4	4
1: Yes					
2: No					
3: Ambiguous: weak assertions or difficult to comprehend					
4: Not Mentioned: Query not applicable or not referred					
** This is the unedited questionnaire that the main text draws on					

	21	22	23	24	25
Article No.					
News Paper	The Tribune	The Indian Express	The Times of India	The Times of India	The Tribune
Author	Megha Mann	Geeta Gupta	-	-	Ashok Tuteja
Length	139	387	417	108	751
Type of Article	News	News	News	News	News
Date	February 23, 2010	February 24, 2010	February 24, 2010	February 25, 2010	February 25, 2010
POLITICAL DISCOURSE					
1 Are unfair/flawed provisions of IWT the reasons for water shortage?	4	4	4	4	4
2 Has regional water shortage led Pakistan to accuse India of breaching water agreements?	4	4	4	4	4
3 Have Pakistan's assertions of India not abiding by the water agreements suggested as being unreasonable?	4	4	4	4	1
4 Should Pakistan and India intensify cooperation to resolve water issues?	4	4	4	4	4
5 Has uneven inter-provincial water distribution/usage been argued to be the cause of water shortage/issue?	4	1	1	4	4
6 Has water shortage led to conflict/disagreement between stakeholders (People, Institutions, Political Parties)?	4	4	1	4	4
7 Has water been employed as a socio-political tool by extremist elements?	4	4	4	4	4
GOVERNANCE					
8 Have administrative lapses or challenges at the local, regional or national level been argued to be the cause of water shortage/issue?	4	1	1	4	4
9 Should public water management/Regulation be improved to solve water shortage?	4	4	4	4	4
10 Has insufficient water/supply provision and storage infrastructure been argued to be the cause of water shortage/issue?	4	1	4	4	4

Article No.	21	22	23	24	25
News Paper	The Tribune	The Indian Express	The Times of India	The Times of India	The Tribune
Author	Megha Mann	Geeta Gupta	-	-	Ashok Tuteja
Length	139	387	417	108	751
Type of Article	News	News	News	News	News
Date	February 23, 2010	February 24, 2010	February 24, 2010	February 25, 2010	February 25, 2010
11 Will investment in water provision/technology provision and storage infrastructure decrease water shortage?	1	1	4	1	4
12 Has public-private partnership/better water pricing partnership been suggested to improve water provision?	4	4	4	4	4
PEOPLE, PRACTICE AND ENVIRONMENT					
13 Have changing climate/rainfall conditions caused water shortage?	4	4	4	4	4
14 Has water shortage led to environmental degradation/issues?	4	4	4	4	4
15 Has underground water been affected?	4	4	4	4	4
16 Has the agricultural/agro dependent rural sector suffered due to water shortage?	4	4	1	3	4
17 Has water shortage affected domestic consumption?	4	4	3	4	4
18 Is crop diversification, or changing cropping patterns a solution to water shortage?	4	4	4	4	4
19 Is training/awareness mentioned as a solution to improve water efficiency ?	4	4	4	4	4

1: Yes
2: No
3: Ambiguous: weak assertions or difficult to comprehend
4: Not Mentioned: Query not applicable or not referred

** This is the unedited questionnaire that the main text draws on

Article No.	26	27	28	29	30
News Paper	The Hindu	The Indian Express	The Hindustan Times	The Indian Express	The Indian Express
Author	-	-	Rajendra Aklekar	B.G. Verghese	Ravish Tiwari
Length	273	250	296	779	679
Type of Article	News	News	News	Comment	News
Date	February 26, 2010	March 06, 2010	March 08, 2010	March 12, 2010	March 12, 2010
POLITICAL DISCOURSE					
1 Are unfair/flawed provisions of IWT the reasons for water shortage?	4	4	4	3	4
2 Has regional water shortage led Pakistan to accuse India of breaching water agreements?	4	1	4	1	1
3 Have Pakistan's assertions of India not abiding by the water agreements suggested as being unreasonable?	4	3	4	1	1
4 Should Pakistan and India intensify cooperation to resolve water issues?	4	1	4	1	1
5 Has uneven inter-provincial water distribution/usage been argued to be the cause of water shortage/issue?	4	4	4	4	4
6 Has water shortage led to conflict/disagreement between stakeholders (People, Institutions, Political Parties)?	4	4	1	4	4
7 Has water been employed as a socio-political tool by extremist elements?	4	4	4	1	1
GOVERNANCE					
8 Have administrative lapses or challenges at the local, regional or national level been argued to be the cause of water shortage/issue?	4	4	1	4	4
9 Should public water management/Regulation be improved to solve water shortage?	1	4	1	4	4
10 Has insufficient water/supply provision and storage infrastructure been argued to be the cause of water shortage/issue?	1	4	4	4	4

Article No.	26	27	28	29	30
News Paper	The Hindu	The Indian Express	The Hindustan Times	The Indian Express	The Indian Express
Author		-	Rajendra Aklekar	B.G. Verghese	Ravish Tiwari
Length	273	250	296	779	679
Type of Article	News	News	News	Comment	News
Date	February 26, 2010	March 06, 2010	March 08, 2010	March 12, 2010	March 12, 2010
11 Will investment in water provision/technology provision and storage infrastructure decrease water shortage?	1	4	4	4	4
12 Has public-private partnership/better water pricing partnership been suggested to improve water provision?	4	4	4	4	4
PEOPLE, PRACTICE AND ENVIRONMENT					
13 Have changing climate/rainfall conditions caused water shortage?	4	4	1	1	4
14 Has water shortage led to environmental degradation/issues?	4	4	4	4	4
15 Has undergound water been affected?	1	4	4	4	4
16 Has the agricultural/agro dependent rural sector suffered due to water shortage?	4	4	4	4	4
17 Has water shortage affected domestic consumption?	4	4	1	4	4
18 Is crop diversification, or changing cropping patterns a solution to water shortage?	4	4	4	4	4
19 Is training/awareness mentioned as a solution to improve water efficiency ?	1	4	4	4	4

1: Yes

2: No

3: Ambiguous: weak assertions or difficult to comprehend

4: Not Mentioned: Query not applicable or not referred

** This is the unedited questionnaire that the main text draws on

Article No.	31	32	33	34	35
News Paper	The Tribune	The Hindustan Times	The Indian Express	The Hindu	The Hindustan Times
Author	Dinesh Manhotra	Bhavika Jain	-	Sandeep Dikshit	-
Length	489	245	472	262	114
Type of Article	News	News	Feature	News	News
Date	March 12, 2010	March 12, 2010	March 13, 2010	March 13, 2010	March 16, 2010
POLITICAL DISCOURSE					
1 Are unfair/flawed provisions of IWT the reasons for water shortage?	4	4	4	3	4
2 Has regional water shortage led Pakistan to accuse India of breaching water agreements?	4	4	4	3	4
3 Have Pakistan's assertions of India not abiding by the water agreements suggested as being unreasonable?	4	4	4	3	4
4 Should Pakistan and India intensify cooperation to resolve water issues?	4	4	4	1	4
5 Has uneven inter-provincial water distribution/usage been argued to be the cause of water shortage/issue?	4	4	4	4	4
6 Has water shortage led to conflict/disagreement between stakeholders (People, Institutions, Political Parties)?	4	4	4	4	4
7 Has water been employed as a socio-political tool by extremist elements?	4	4	4	4	4
GOVERNANCE					
8 Have administrative lapses or challenges at the local, regional or national level been argued to be the cause of water shortage/issue?	4	4	4	4	4
9 Should public water management/Regulation be improved to solve water shortage?	4	4	4	4	4
10 Has insufficient water/supply provision and storage infrastructure been argued to be the cause of water shortage/issue?	4	4	4	4	1

Article No.	31	32	33	34	35
News Paper	The Tribune	The Hindustan Times	The Indian Express	The Hindu	The Hindustan Times
Author	Dinesh Manhotra	Bhavika Jain	-	Sandeep Dikshit	-
Length	489	245	472	262	114
Type of Article	News	News	Feature	News	News
Date	March 12, 2010	March 12, 2010	March 13, 2010	March 13, 2010	March 16, 2010
11 Will investment in water provision/technology provision and storage infrastructure decrease water shortage?	1	4	4	4	3
12 Has public-private partnership/better water pricing partnership been suggested to improve water provision?	4	4	4	4	4
PEOPLE, PRACTICE AND ENVIRONMENT					
13 Have changing climate/rainfall conditions caused water shortage?	1	4	1	4	4
14 Has water shortage led to environmental degradation/issues?	4	4	4	1	4
15 Has underground water been affected?	1	1	4	4	4
16 Has the agricultural/agro dependent rural sector suffered due to water shortage?	4	4	1	4	4
17 Has water shortage affected domestic consumption?	1	4	4	4	4
18 Is crop diversification, or changing cropping patterns a solution to water shortage?	4	4	4	4	4
19 Is training/awareness mentioned as a solution to improve water efficiency ?	4	4	4	4	4
1: Yes					
2: No					
3: Ambiguous: weak assertions or difficult to comprehend					
4: Not Mentioned: Query not applicable or not referred					
** This is the unedited questionnaire that the main text draws on					

Article No.	36	37	38	39	40
News Paper	The Times of India	The Tribune	The Times of India	The Hindu	The Telegraph
Author	-	Neena Sharma	Akhilesh Sourav Jha	K. Raju	SHASHANK SHEKHAR
Length	464	287	334	92	410
Type of Article	News	News	News	News	News
Date	March 17, 2010	March 17, 2010	March 18, 2010	March 18, 2010	March 18, 2010
POLITICAL DISCOURSE					
1 Are unfair/flawed provisions of IWT the reasons for water shortage?	4	4	4	4	4
2 Has regional water shortage led Pakistan to accuse India of breaching water agreements?	4	4	4	4	4
3 Have Pakistan's assertions of India not abiding by the water agreements suggested as being unreasonable?	4	4	4	4	4
4 Should Pakistan and India intensify cooperation to resolve water issues?	4	4	4	4	4
5 Has uneven inter-provincial water distribution/usage been argued to be the cause of water shortage/issue?	4	4	4	4	4
6 Has water shortage led to conflict/disagreement between stakeholders (People, Institutions, Political Parties)?	1	4	4	4	4
7 Has water been employed as a socio-political tool by extremist elements?	4	4	4	4	4
GOVERNANCE					
8 Have administrative lapses or challenges at the local, regional or national level been argued to be the cause of water shortage/issue?	4	3	1	1	1
9 Should public water management/Regulation be improved to solve water shortage?	4	1	1	1	3
10 Has insufficient water/supply provision and storage infrastructure been argued to be the cause of water shortage/issue?	1	3	1	4	1

Article No.	36	37	38	39	40
News Paper	The Times of India	The Tribune	The Times of India	The Hindu	The Telegraph
Author	-	Neena Sharma	Akhilesh Sourav Jha	K. Raju	SHASHANK SHEKHAR
Length	464	287	334	92	410
Type of Article	News	News	News	News	News
Date	March 17, 2010	March 17, 2010	March 18, 2010	March 18, 2010	March 18, 2010
11 Will investment in water provision/technology provision and storage infrastructure decrease water shortage?	1	1	1	4	1
12 Has public-private partnership/better water pricing partnership been suggested to improve water provision?	4	4	4	4	4
PEOPLE, PRACTICE AND ENVIRONMENT					
13 Have changing climate/rainfall conditions caused water shortage?	4	1	4	1	4
14 Has water shortage led to environmental degradation/issues?	4	4	4	4	4
15 Has undergound water been affected?	4	4	4	4	1
16 Has the agricultural/agro dependent rural sector suffered due to water shortage?	4	3	4	1	4
17 Has water shortage affected domestic consumption?	1	1	4	4	1
18 Is crop diversification, or changing cropping patterns a solution to water shortage?	4	4	4	4	4
19 Is training/awareness mentioned as a solution to improve water efficiency ?	4	4	4	4	4
1: Yes					
2: No					
3: Ambiguous: weak assertions or difficult to comprehend					
4: Not Mentioned: Query not applicable or not referred					
** This is the unedited questionnaire that the main text draws on					

Article No.	41	42	43	44	45
News Paper	The Times of India	The Times of India	The Indian Express	The Times of India	The Telegraph
Author	Sukhada Tatke	Sunil Mungara	-	P J Joychen & Akhilesh Saurav Jha	-
Length	449	429	443	431	501
Type of Article	News	News	News	News	News
Date	March 20, 2010	March 21, 2010	March 22, 2010	March 22, 2010	March 22, 2010
POLITICAL DISCOURSE					
1 Are unfair/flawed provisions of IWT the reasons for water shortage?	4	4	4	4	4
2 Has regional water shortage led Pakistan to accuse India of breaching water agreements?	4	4	4	4	4
3 Have Pakistan's assertions of India not abiding by the water agreements suggested as being unreasonable?	4	4	4	4	4
4 Should Pakistan and India intensify cooperation to resolve water issues?	4	4	4	4	4
5 Has uneven inter-provincial water distribution/usage been argued to be the cause of water shortage/issue?	4	4	4	4	4
6 Has water shortage led to conflict/disagreement between stakeholders (People, Institutions, Political Parties)?	4	4	1	4	4
7 Has water been employed as a socio-political tool by extremist elements?	4	4	4	4	4
GOVERNANCE					
8 Have administrative lapses or challenges at the local, regional or national level been argued to be the cause of water shortage/issue?	4	4	4	4	4
9 Should public water management/Regulation be improved to solve water shortage?	4	4	4	4	4
10 Has insufficient water/supply provision and storage infrastructure been argued to be the cause of water shortage/issue?	1	4	4	1	4

	41	42	43	44	45
Article No.					
News Paper	The Times of India	The Times of India	The Indian Express	The Times of India	The Telegraph
Author	Sukhada Tatke	Sunil Mungara	-	P J Joychen & Akhilesh Saurav Jha	-
Length	449	429	443	431	501
Type of Article	News	News	News	News	News
Date	March 20, 2010	March 21, 2010	March 22, 2010	March 22, 2010	March 22, 2010
11 Will investment in water provision/technology provision and storage infrastructure decrease water shortage?	1	4	4	4	4
12 Has public-private partnership/better water pricing partnership been suggested to improve water provision?	4	4	4	4	4
PEOPLE, PRACTICE AND ENVIRONMENT					
13 Have changing climate/rainfall conditions caused water shortage?	4	4	4	1	1
14 Has water shortage led to environmental degradation/issues?	4	4	1	4	4
15 Has undergound water been affected?	1	1	1	4	1
16 Has the agricultural/agro dependent rural sector suffered due to water shortage?	4	4	4	4	4
17 Has water shortage affected domestic consumption?	1	1	4	1	3
18 Is crop diversification, or changing cropping patterns a solution to water shortage?	4	4	4	4	4
19 Is training/awareness mentioned as a solution to improve water efficiency ?	4	4	4	4	4
1: Yes					
2: No					
3: Ambiguous: weak assertions or difficult to comprehend					
4: Not Mentioned: Query not applicable or not referred					
** This is the unedited questionnaire that the main text draws on					

Article No.	46	47	48	49	50
News Paper	The Times of India	The Tribune	The Hindu	The Times of India	The Hindu
Author	Rachna Singh	N Ravikumar/TNS	Gollapudi Srinivasa Rao	-	K. Lakshmi
Length	337	243	316	372	217
Type of Article	News	News	News	Feature	News
Date	March 23, 2010	March 23, 2010	March 25, 2010	March 29, 2010	March 31, 2010
POLITICAL DISCOURSE					
1 Are unfair/flawed provisions of IWT the reasons for water shortage?	4	4	4	4	4
2 Has regional water shortage led Pakistan to accuse India of breaching water agreements?	4	4	4	4	4
3 Have Pakistan's assertions of India not abiding by the water agreements suggested as being unreasonable?	4	4	4	4	4
4 Should Pakistan and India intensify cooperation to resolve water issues?	4	4	4	4	4
5 Has uneven inter-provincial water distribution/usage been argued to be the cause of water shortage/issue?	4	1	4	4	4
6 Has water shortage led to conflict/disagreement between stakeholders (People, Institutions, Political Parties)?	4	1	4	4	4
7 Has water been employed as a socio-political tool by extremist elements?	4	4	4	4	4
GOVERNANCE					
8 Have administrative lapses or challenges at the local, regional or national level been argued to be the cause of water shortage/issue?	4	4	3	3	4
9 Should public water management/Regulation be improved to solve water shortage?	4	4	4	1	4
10 Has insufficient water/supply provision and storage infrastructure been argued to be the cause of water shortage/issue?	4	4	3	3	4

		46	47	48	49	50
Article No.		46	47	48	49	50
News Paper		The Times of India	The Tribune	The Hindu	The Times of India	The Hindu
Author		Rachna Singh	N Ravikumar/TNS	Gollapudi Srinivasa Rao	-	K. Lakshmi
Length		337	243	316	372	217
Type of Article		News	News	News	Feature	News
Date		March 23, 2010	March 23, 2010	March 25, 2010	March 29, 2010	March 31, 2010
11	Will investment in water provision/technology provision and storage infrastructure decrease water shortage?	3	4	3	1	1
12	Has public-private partnership/better water pricing partnership been suggested to improve water provision?	4	4	4	4	4
PEOPLE, PRACTICE AND ENVIRONMENT						
13	Have changing climate/rainfall conditions caused water shortage?	4	4	4	1	1
14	Has water shortage led to environmental degradation/issues?	4	4	1	4	4
15	Has undergound water been affected?	1	1	1	4	1
16	Has the agricultural/agro dependent rural sector suffered due to water shortage?	4	4	4	4	4
17	Has water shortage affected domestic consumption?	1	1	4	1	3
18	Is crop diversification, or changing cropping patterns a solution to water shortage?	4	4	4	4	4
19	Is training/awareness mentioned as a solution to improve water efficiency ?	4	4	4	4	4
	1: Yes					
	2: No					
	3: Ambiguous: weak assertions or difficult to comprehend					
	4: Not Mentioned: Query not applicable or not referred					
	** This is the unedited questionnaire that the main text draws on					

Pakistan Spring

Article No.	01	02	03	04	05
News Paper	The Nation	The Daily Times	The Dawn	The Nation	The Dawn
Author	Khalid Malik	-	Ashfak Bokhari	-	Rehan Ali
Length	247	159	1143	343	841
Type of Article	News	News	Feature	Editorial	Feature
Date	April 02, 2010	April 05, 2010	April 05, 2010	April 05, 2010	April 11, 2010
POLITICAL DISCOURSE					
1 Has the IWT been put forth as the reason for water shortage/challenge?	4	4	1	4	4
2 Has Indian action and/or transgression been presented as a reason for water shortage/challenge?	4	4	1	1	4
3 Has political pressure against India been presented as a solution to water shortage?	4	4	1	3	4
4 Has water shortage led to negative sentiments towards India?	4	4	1	4	4
5 Has increased cooperation between Pakistan and India been presented as a solution to water issues?	4	4	1	3	4
6 Has water shortage led to conflict between stakeholders (People, institutions, political parties)?	4	4	4	4	4
7 Has inter-provincial water distribution/unfair implementation of domestic water sharing accord been argued to be the cause of water shortage?	4	4		4	4
8 Implementation of domestic water sharing arrangements in letter and spirit	4	4	4	4	4

Article No.	01	02	03	04	05
News Paper	The Nation	The Daily Times	The Dawn	The Nation	The Dawn
Author	Khalid Malik	-	Ashfak Bokhari	-	Rehan Ali
Length	247	159	1143	343	841
Type of Article	News	News	Feature	Editorial	Feature
Date	April 02, 2010	April 05, 2010	April 05, 2010	April 05, 2010	April 11, 2010
GOVERNANCE					
9 Have administrative lapses or challenges at the local, regional or national level been argued to be the cause of water shortage?	1	4	3	4	1
10 Should public water management be improved to solve water shortage?	1	4	3	4	1
11 Has insufficient water provision and storage infrastructure been argued to be the cause of water shortage?	1	4	1	4	4
12 Will investment/attention/technology solutions to water provision and storage infrastructure decrease water shortage?	1	4	4	4	1
PEOPLE, PRACTICE AND ENVIRONMENT					
13 Have changing climate/rainfall conditions caused water shortage?	4	4	1	4	4
14 Has water shortage led to environmental degradation?	4	4	4	4	4
15 Has undergound water been affected?	4	4	4	4	3
16 Has the agricultural/agro dependent rural sector suffered due to water shortage?	4	1	1	4	4
17 Has water shortage affected domestic consumption?	1	1	4	4	1
18 Is crop diversification, or changing cropping patterns a solution to water shortage?	4	4	4	4	4
19 Is training/awareness mentioned as a solution to improve water efficiency ?	4	4	4	4	4

1: Yes

2: No

3: Ambiguous: weak assertions or difficult to comprehend

4: Not Mentioned: Query not applicable or not referred

** This is the unedited questionnaire that the main text draws on

	06	07	08	09	10
News Paper	The Nation	The Daily Times	The Daily Times	The Dawn	The Daily Times
Author	-	-	-	Mohammad Hussain Khan	-
Length	117	522	405	656	277
Type of Article	News	News	News	News	News
Date	April 11, 2010	April 13, 2010	April 14, 2010	April 15, 2010	April 24, 2010
POLITICAL DISCOURSE					
1 Has the IWT been put forth as the reason for water shortage/challenge?	4	4	4	4	4
2 Has Indian action and/or transgression been presented as a reason for water shortage/challenge?	4	4	4	4	4
3 Has political pressure against India been presented as a solution to water shortage?	4	4	4	4	4
4 Has water shortage led to negative sentiments towards India?	4	4	4	4	4
5 Has the increased cooperation between Pakistan and India been presented as a solution to water issues?	4	4	4	4	4
6 Has water shortage led to conflict between stakeholders (People, institutions, political parties)?	4	4	4	1	4
7 Has inter-provincial water distribution/unfair implementation of domestic water sharing accord been argued to be the cause of water shortage?	4	4	4	1	4
8 Implementation of domestic water sharing arrangements in letter and spirit	4	4	4	4	4

Article No.	06	07	08	09	10
News Paper	The Nation	The Daily Times	The Daily Times	The Dawn	The Daily Times
Author	-	-	-	Mohammad Hussain Khan	-
Length	117	522	405	656	277
Type of Article	News	News	News	News	News
Date	April 11, 2010	April 13, 2010	April 14, 2010	April 15, 2010	April 24, 2010
GOVERNANCE					
9 Have administrative lapses or challenges at the local, regional or national level been argued to be the cause of water shortage?	4	4	4	3	4
10 Should public water management be improved to solve water shortage?	4	4	4	3	4
11 Has insufficient water provision and storage infrastructure been argued to be the cause of water shortage?	4	4	4	4	4
12 Will investment/attention/technology solutions to water provision and storage infrastructure decrease water shortage?	4	1	1	4	4
PEOPLE, PRACTICE AND ENVIRONMENT					
13 Have changing climate/rainfall conditions caused water shortage?	1	4	4	4	4
14 Has water shortage led to environmental degradation?	4	4	4	4	4
15 Has underground water been affected?	4	4	4	4	4
16 Has the agricultural/agro dependent rural sector suffered due to water shortage?	4	4	1	1	1
17 Has water shortage affected domestic consumption?	4	4	4	4	4
18 Is crop diversification, or changing cropping patterns a solution to water shortage?	4	4	1	4	4
19 Is training/awareness mentioned as a solution to improve water efficiency ?	4	4	1	4	4

1: Yes

2: No

3: Ambiguous: weak assertions or difficult to comprehend

4: Not Mentioned: Query not applicable or not referred

** This is the unedited questionnaire that the main text draws on

Article No.	11	12	13	14	15
News Paper	The Dawn	The Dawn	The Nation	The Pak Tribune	The Pak Tribune
Author	-	A. B. Arisar	-	-	Zaheerul Hassan
Length	350	625	266	512	1242
Type of Article	Editorial	News	News	News	Feature
Date	April 24, 2010	April 26, 2010	April 26, 2010	April 26, 2010	April 28, 2010
POLITICAL DISCOURSE					
1 Has the IWT been put forth as the reason for water shortage/challenge?	4	4	4	4	4
2 Has Indian action and/or transgression been presented as a reason for water shortage/ challenge?	4	4	4	4	1
3 Has political pressure against India been presented as a solution to water shortage?	4	4	4	4	1
4 Has water shortage led to negative sentiments towards India?	4	4	4	4	1
5 Has the increased cooperation between Pakistan and India been presented as a solution to water issues?	4	4	3	3	3
6 Has water shortage led to conflict between stakeholders (People, institutions, political parties)?	4	4	4	4	4
7 Has inter-provincial water distribution/unfair implementation of domestic water sharing accord been argued to be the cause of water shortage?	1	3	4	4	4
8 Implementation of domestic water sharing arrangements in letter and spirit	1	4	4	4	4

Article No.	11	12	13	14	15
News Paper	The Dawn	The Dawn	The Nation	The Pak Tribune	The Pak Tribune
Author	-	A. B. Arisar	-	-	Zaheerul Hassan
Length	350	625	266	512	1242
Type of Article	Editorial	News	News	News	Feature
Date	April 24, 2010	April 26, 2010	April 26, 2010	April 26, 2010	April 28, 2010
GOVERNANCE					
9 Have administrative lapses or challenges at the local, regional or national level been argued to be the cause of water shortage?	1	4	4	4	4
10 Should public water management be improved to solve water shortage?	1	4	4	4	4
11 Has insufficient water provision and storage infrastructure been argued to be the cause of water shortage?	4	4	4	4	4
12 Will investment/attention/technology solutions to water provision and storage infrastructure decrease water shortage?	1	4	4	4	4
PEOPLE, PRACTICE AND ENVIRONMENT					
13 Have changing climate/rainfall conditions caused water shortage?	4	4	4	4	4
14 Has water shortage led to environmental degradation?	4	4	4	4	1
15 Has underground water been affected?	4	4	4	4	4
16 Has the agricultural/agro dependent rural sector suffered due to water shortage?	4	1	4	4	1
17 Has water shortage affected domestic consumption?	4	4	4	4	1
18 Is crop diversification, or changing cropping patterns a solution to water shortage?	4	1	4	4	4
19 Is training/awareness mentioned as a solution to improve water efficiency ?	4	1	4	4	4
1: Yes					
2: No					
3: Ambiguous: weak assertions or difficult to comprehend					
4: Not Mentioned: Query not applicable or not referred					
** This is the unedited questionnaire that the main text draws on					

	16	17	18	19	20
Article No.					
News Paper	The Pak Tribune	The Dawn	The Dawn	The Nation	The Dawn
Author	-	Mansoor Mirani	Khaleeq Kiani	-	Qamaruddin
Length	1212	467	686	338	299
Type of Article	News	News	Feature	News	News
Date	April 29, 2010	May 01, 2010	May 03, 2010	May 03, 2010	May 05, 2010

POLITICAL DISCOURSE

		16	17	18	19	20
1	Has the IWT been put forth as the reason for water shortage/challenge?	4	4	4	1	4
2	Has Indian action and/or transgression been presented as a reason for water shortage/challenge?	4	4	1	1	4
3	Has political pressure against India been presented as a solution to water shortage?	4	4	1	1	4
4	Has water shortage led to negative sentiments towards India?	4	4	4	1	4
5	Has the increased cooperation between Pakistan and India been presented as a solution to water issues?	1	4	3	3	4
6	Has water shortage led to conflict between stakeholders (People, institutions, political parties)?	4	3	4	4	3
7	Has inter-provincial water distribution/unfair implementation of domestic water sharing accord been argued to be the cause of water shortage?	4	4	4	4	4
8	Implementation of domestic water sharing arrangements in letter and spirit	4	4	4	4	4

Article No.	16	17	18	19	20
News Paper	The Pak Tribune	The Dawn	The Dawn	The Nation	The Dawn
Author	-	Mansoor Mirani	Khaleeq Kiani	-	Qamaruddin
Length	1212	467	686	338	299
Type of Article	News	News	Feature	News	News
Date	April 29, 2010	May 01, 2010	May 03, 2010	May 03, 2010	May 05, 2010
GOVERNANCE					
9 Have administrative lapses or challenges at the local, regional or national level been argued to be the cause of water shortage?	4	1	4	4	1
10 Should public water management be improved to solve water shortage?	4	1	4	4	1
11 Has insufficient water provision and storage infrastructure been argued to be the cause of water shortage?	4	4	4	4	4
12 Will investment/attention/technology solutions to water provision and storage infrastructure decrease water shortage?	4	4	4	4	1
PEOPLE, PRACTICE AND ENVIRONMENT					
13 Have changing climate/rainfall conditions caused water shortage?	4	4	4	4	4
14 Has water shortage led to environmental degradation?	4	4	4	4	4
15 Has undergound water been affected?	4	4	4	4	4
16 Has the agricultural/agro dependent rural sector suffered due to water shortage?	4	1	4	1	1
17 Has water shortage affected domestic consumption?	4	4	4	4	4
18 Is crop diversification, or changing cropping patterns a solution to water shortage?	4	4	4	4	4
19 Is training/awareness mentioned as a solution to improve water efficiency ?	4	4	4	4	4

1: Yes

2: No

3: Ambiguous: weak assertions or difficult to comprehend

4: Not Mentioned: Query not applicable or not referred

** This is the unedited questionnaire that the main text draws on

Article No.	21	22	23	24	25
News Paper	The Nation	Pakistan Observer	The Nation	The Daily Times	The Dawn
Author	-	Shah Hasan	-	-	Aamir Yasin
Length	288	465	382	78	487
Type of Article	News	Feature	Editorial	News	News
Date	May 10, 2010	May 11, 2010	May 13, 2010	May 14, 2010	May 14, 2010
POLITICAL DISCOURSE					
1 Has the IWT been put forth as the reason for water shortage/challenge?	4	4	4	4	4
2 Has Indian action and/or transgression been presented as a reason for water shortage/challenge?	4	4	1	4	4
3 Has political pressure against India been presented as a solution to water shortage?	4	4	3	4	4
4 Has water shortage led to negative sentiments towards India?	4	4	1	4	4
5 Has the increased cooperation between Pakistan and India been presented as a solution to water issues?	3	4	3	4	4
6 Has water shortage led to conflict between stakeholders (People, institutions, political parties)?	4	3	4	1	3
7 Has inter-provincial water distribution/unfair implementation of domestic water sharing accord been argued to be the cause of water shortage?	4	4	4	4	4
8 Implementation of domestic water sharing arrangements in letter and spirit	4	4	4	4	4

Article No.	21	22	23	24	25
News Paper	The Nation	Pakistan Observer	The Nation	The Daily Times	The Dawn
Author	-	Shah Hasan	-	-	Aamir Yasin
Length	288	465	382	78	487
Type of Article	News	Feature	Editorial	News	News
Date	May 10, 2010	May 11, 2010	May 13, 2010	May 14, 2010	May 14, 2010

GOVERNANCE

	21	22	23	24	25
9 Have administrative lapses or challenges at the local, regional or national level been argued to be the cause of water shortage?	4	1	1	4	1
10 Should public water management be improved to solve water shortage?	4	1	4	4	1
11 Has insufficient water provision and storage infrastructure been argued to be the cause of water shortage?	4	4	4	4	4
12 Will investment/attention/technology solutions to water provision and storage infrastructure decrease water shortage?	4	4	1	4	4

PEOPLE, PRACTICE AND ENVIRONMENT

	21	22	23	24	25
13 Have changing climate/rainfall conditions caused water shortage?	4	4	4	4	4
14 Has water shortage led to environmental degradation?	4	4	4	4	4
15 Has underground water been affected?	4	4	4	4	4
16 Has the agricultural/agro dependent rural sector suffered due to water shortage?	1	1	1	4	4
17 Has water shortage affected domestic consumption?	4	4	1	4	1
18 Is crop diversification, or changing cropping patterns a solution to water shortage?	4	4	4	4	4
19 Is training/awareness mentioned as a solution to improve water efficiency ?	4	4	4	4	4

1: Yes
2: No
3: Ambiguous: weak assertions or difficult to comprehend
4: Not Mentioned: Query not applicable or not referred

** This is the unedited questionnaire that the main text draws on

Article No.	26	27	28	29	30
News Paper	The Dawn	The Dawn	Pakistan Observer	The Nation	Pakistan Observer
Author	Iqbal Khwaja	Dr Charles K. Ebinger & Kashif Hasnie	-	Ramzan Chandio	Ghazanfar Ali Astori
Length	364	816	191	233	147
Type of Article	News	Feature	News	News	Comment
Date	May 16, 2010	May 17, 2010	May 24, 2010	May 25, 2010	May 26, 2010
POLITICAL DISCOURSE					
1 Has the IWT been put forth as the reason for water shortage/challenge?	4	4	4	4	4
2 Has Indian action and/or transgression been presented as a reason for water shortage/challenge?	4	4	4	4	4
3 Has political pressure against India been presented as a solution to water shortage?	4	4	4	4	4
4 Has water shortage led to negative sentiments towards India?	4	4	4	4	4
5 Has the increased cooperation between Pakistan and India been presented as a soultion to water issues?	4	4	4	4	4
6 Has water shortage lead to conflict between stakeholders (People, institutions, political parties)?	4	4	4	1	4
7 Has inter-provincial water distribution/unfair implementation of domestic water sharing accord been argued to be the cause of water shortage?	4	1	4	1	4
8 Implementation of domestic water sharing arrangements in letter and spirit	4	4	4	1	4

	26	27	28	29	30
News Paper	The Dawn	The Dawn	Pakistan Observer	The Nation	Pakistan Observer
Author	Iqbal Khwaja	Dr Charles K. Ebinger & Kashif Hasnie	-	Ramzan Chandio	Ghazanfar Ali Astori
Length	364	816	191	233	147
Type of Article	News	Feature	News	News	Comment
Date	May 16, 2010	May 17, 2010	May 24, 2010	May 25, 2010	May 26, 2010

GOVERNANCE

	26	27	28	29	30
9. Have administrative lapses or challenges at the local, regional or national level been argued to be the cause of water shortage?	1	1	4	1	1
10. Should public water management be improved to solve water shortage?	1	1	4	1	1
11. Has insufficient water provision and storage infrastructure been argued to be the cause of water shortage?	4	4	4	4	1
12. Will investment/attention/technology solutions to water provision and storage infrastructure decrease water shortage?	4	1	4	4	1

PEOPLE, PRACTICE AND ENVIRONMENT

	26	27	28	29	30
13. Have changing climate/rainfall conditions caused water shortage?	4	1	4	4	4
14. Has water shortage led to environmental degradation?	4	4	4	4	4
15. Has underground water been affected?	4	4	4	4	4
16. Has the agricultural/agro dependent rural sector suffered due to water shortage?	1	3	4	1	4
17. Has water shortage affected domestic consumption?	1	4	1	1	1
18. Is crop diversification, or changing cropping patterns a solution to water shortage?	4	4	4	4	4
19. Is training/awareness mentioned as a solution to improve water efficiency ?	4	4	4	4	4

1: Yes
2: No
3: Ambiguous: weak assertions or difficult to comprehend
4: Not Mentioned: Query not applicable or not referred

** This is the unedited questionnaire that the main text draws on

Article No.	31	32	33	34	35
News Paper	The Daily Times	The Nation	The Nation	The Pak Tribune	The Daily Times
Author	Zeeshan Javaid	S.m. Hali	-	-	Razi Syed
Length	387	329	226	445	587
Type of Article	News	Comment	News	News	News
Date	May 26, 2010	May 26, 2010	May 26, 2010	May 29, 2010	May 30, 2010
POLITICAL DISCOURSE					
1 Has the IWT been put forth as the reason for water shortage/challenge?	4	4	4	4	4
2 Has Indian action and/or transgression been presented as a reason for water shortage/challenge?	4	1	4	4	4
3 Has political pressure against India been presented as a solution to water shortage?	4	3	4	4	4
4 Has water shortage led to negative sentiments towards India?	4	1	4	4	4
5 Has the increased cooperation between Pakistan and India been presented as a solution to water issues?	4	3	4	4	4
6 Has water shortage lead to conflict between stakeholders (People, institutions, political parties)?	3	4	4	1	1
7 Has inter-provincial water distribution/unfair implementation of domestic water sharing accord been argued to be the cause of water shortage?	1	4	4	1	1
8 Implementation of domestic water sharing arrangements in letter and spirit	4	4	4	4	4

Article No.	31	32	33	34	35
News Paper	The Daily Times	The Nation	The Nation	The Pak Tribune	The Daily Times
Author	Zeeshan Javaid	S.m. Hali	-	-	Razi Syed
Length	387	329	226	445	587
Type of Article	News	Comment	News	News	News
Date	May 26, 2010	May 26, 2010	May 26, 2010	May 29, 2010	May 30, 2010
GOVERNANCE					
9 Have administrative lapses or challenges at the local, regional or national level been argued to be the cause of water shortage?	4	4	4	4	4
10 Should public water management be improved to solve water shortage?	4	4	4	4	4
11 Has insufficient water provision and storage infrastructure been argued to be the cause of water shortage?	4	4	4	4	4
12 Will investment/attention/technology solutions to water provision and storage infrastructure decrease water shortage?	4	4	1	4	4
PEOPLE, PRACTICE AND ENVIRONMENT					
13 Have changing climate/rainfall conditions caused water shortage?	4	1	4	4	4
14 Has water shortage led to environmental degradation?	4	1	4	4	4
15 Has undergound water been affected?	4	4	4	4	4
16 Has the agricultural/agro dependent rural sector suffered due to water shortage?	4	1	4	1	1
17 Has water shortage affected domestic consumption?	4	1	4	4	4
18 Is crop diversification, or changing cropping patterns a solution to water shortage?	4	4	4	4	4
19 Is training/awareness mentioned as a solution to improve water efficiency ?	4	4	4	4	4
1: Yes					
2: No					
3: Ambiguous: weak assertions or difficult to comprehend					
4: Not Mentioned: Query not applicable or not referred					
** This is the unedited questionnaire that the main text draws on					

Article No.		36	37	38	39	40
News Paper		The Pak Tribune	The Dawn	Pakistan Observer	The Nation	The Dawn
Author		-	-	-	Kaswar Klasra	Amin Ahmed
Length		439	364	88	301	418
Type of Article		News	News	News	News	News
Date		May 31, 2010	June 01, 2010	June 02, 2010	June 04, 2010	June 05, 2010
POLITICAL DISCOURSE						
1	Has the IWT been put forth as the reason for water shortage/challenge?	4	4	4	4	4
2	Has Indian action and/or transgression been presented as a reason for water shortage/ challenge?	3	4	1	1	4
3	Has political pressure against India been presented as a solution to water shortage?	4	4	3	4	4
4	Has water shortage led to negative sentiments towards India?	4	4	4	4	4
5	Has the increased cooperation between Pakistan and India been presented as a solution to water issues?	1	4	3	1	4
6	Has water shortage lead to conflict between stakeholders (People, institutions, political parties)?	4	1	4	4	4
7	Has inter-provincial water distribution/unfair implementation of domestic water sharing accord been argued to be the cause of water shortage?	4	1	4	4	4
8	Implementation of domestic water sharing arrangements in letter and spirit	4	4	4	4	4

Article No.	36	37	38	39	40
News Paper	The Pak Tribune	The Dawn	Pakistan Observer	The Nation	The Dawn
Author	-	-	-	Kaswar Klasra	Amin Ahmed
Length	439	364	88	301	418
Type of Article	News	News	News	News	News
Date	May 31, 2010	June 01, 2010	June 02, 2010	June 04, 2010	June 05, 2010
GOVERNANCE					
9 Have administrative lapses or challenges at the local, regional or national level been argued to be the cause of water shortage?	1	4	4	4	4
10 Should public water management be improved to solve water shortage?	4	4	4	4	4
11 Has insufficient water provision and storage infrastructure been argued to be the cause of water shortage?	4	4	4	4	4
12 Will investment/attention/technology solutions to water provision and storage infrastructure decrease water shortage?	4	4	4	4	4
PEOPLE, PRACTICE AND ENVIRONMENT					
13 Have changing climate/rainfall conditions caused water shortage?	4	4	4	4	1
14 Has water shortage led to environmental degradation?	4	4	4	4	4
15 Has undergound water been affected?	4	1	1	4	4
16 Has the agricultural/agro dependent rural sector suffered due to water shortage?	4	1	4	4	1
17 Has water shortage affected domestic consumption?	4	1	4	4	4
18 Is crop diversification, or changing cropping patterns a solution to water shortage?	4	4	4	4	4
19 Is training/awareness mentioned as a solution to improve water efficiency ?	4	4	4	4	4

1: Yes

2: No

3: Ambiguous: weak assertions or difficult to comprehend

4: Not Mentioned: Query not applicable or not referred

** This is the unedited questionnaire that the main text draws on

Article No.	41	42	43	44	45
News Paper	Pakistan Observer	The Nation	The Dawn	The Dawn	The Pak Tribune
Author	Lubna Umar	Javaid-ur-rahman	-	-	-
Length	1289	380	287	424	225
Type of Article	Comment	News	News	News	News
Date	June 08, 2010	June 14, 2010	June 15, 2010	June 16, 2010	June 18, 2010

POLITICAL DISCOURSE

		41	42	43	44	45
1	Has the IWT been put forth as the reason for water shortage/challenge?	4	4	4	4	4
2	Has Indian action and/or transgression been presented as a reason for water shortage/challenge?	1	4	4	4	4
3	Has political pressure against India been presented as a solution to water shortage?	1	4	4	4	4
4	Has water shortage led to negative sentiments towards between India?	1	4	4	4	4
5	Has the increased cooperation between Pakistan and India been presented as a solution to water issues?	3	4	4	4	4
6	Has water shortage led to conflict between stakeholders (People, institutions, political parties)?	4	4	1	1	4
7	Has inter-provincial water distribution/unfair implementation of domestic water sharing accord been argued to be the cause of water shortage?	1	4	4	1	1
8	Implementation of domestic water sharing arrangements in letter and spirit	4	4	4	4	4

Article No.	41	42	43	44	45
News Paper	Pakistan Observer	The Nation	The Dawn	The Dawn	The Pak Tribune
Author	Lubna Umar	Javaid-ur-rahman	-	-	-
Length	1289	380	287	424	225
Type of Article	Comment	News	News	News	News
Date	June 08, 2010	June 14, 2010	June 15, 2010	June 16, 2010	June 18, 2010
GOVERNANCE					
9 Have administrative lapses or challenges at the local, regional or national level been argued to be the cause of water shortage?	1	4	4	1	1
10 Should public water management be improved to solve water shortage?	4	4	1	1	1
11 Has insufficient water provision and storage infrastructure been argued to be the cause of water shortage?	1	4	4	4	4
12 Will investment/attention/technology solutions to water provision and storage infrastructure decrease water shortage?	4	1	4	4	4
PEOPLE, PRACTICE AND ENVIRONMENT					
13 Have changing climate/rainfall conditions caused water shortage?	4	4	4	4	4
14 Has water shortage led to environmental degradation?	4	4	4	4	4
15 Has underground water been affected?	4	4	1	4	4
16 Has the agricultural/agro dependent rural sector suffered due to water shortage?	1	1	1	1	4
17 Has water shortage affected domestic consumption?	4	4	1	1	4
18 Is crop diversification, or changing cropping patterns a solution to water shortage?	4	4	4	4	4
19 Is training/awareness mentioned as a solution to improve water efficiency ?	4	4	4	4	4

1: Yes
2: No
3: Ambiguous: weak assertions or difficult to comprehend
4: Not Mentioned: Query not applicable or not referred

** This is the unedited questionnaire that the main text draws on

Article No.	46	47	48	49	50
News Paper	The Dawn	The Pak Tribune	Pakistan Observer	Pakistan Observer	The Daily Times
Author	-	-	Shah Hasan	-	Ijaz Kakakhel
Length	491	409	315	322	659
Type of Article	News	News	News	Editorial	News
Date	June 19, 2010	June 19, 2010	June 25, 2010	June 26, 2010	June 27, 2010
POLITICAL DISCOURSE					
1 Has the IWT been put forth as the reason for water shortage/challenge?	4	4	4	4	4
2 Has Indian action and/or transgression been presented as a reason for water shortage/challenge?	4	4	4	1	4
3 Has political pressure against India been presented as a solution to water shortage?	4	4	4	3	4
4 Has water shortage led to negative sentiments towards India?	4	4	4	4	4
5 Has the increased cooperation between Pakistan and India been presented as a solution to water issues?	4	4	4	4	4
6 Has water shortage lead to conflict between stakeholders (People, institutions, political parties)?	1	1	4	4	4
7 Has inter-provincial water distribution/unfair implementation of domestic water sharing accord been argued to be the cause of water shortage?	4	1	4	4	4
8 Implementation of domestic water sharing arrangements in letter and spirit	4	1	4	4	4

Article No.	46	47	48	49	50
News Paper	The Dawn	The Pak Tribune	Pakistan Observer	Pakistan Observer	The Daily Times
Author	-	-	Shah Hasan	-	Ijaz Kakakhel
Length	491	409	315	322	659
Type of Article	News	News	News	Editorial	News
Date	June 19, 2010	June 19, 2010	June 25, 2010	June 26, 2010	June 27, 2010
GOVERNANCE					
9 Have administrative lapses or challenges at the local, regional or national level been argued to be the cause of water shortage?	1	4	4	1	1
10 Should public water management be improved to solve water shortage?	1	4	4	1	1
11 Has insufficient water provision and storage infrastructure been argued to be the cause of water shortage?	4	4	1	1	1
12 Will investment/attention/technology solutions to water provision and storage infrastructure decrease water shortage?	4	4	1	1	1
PEOPLE, PRACTICE AND ENVIRONMENT					
13 Have changing climate/rainfall conditions caused water shortage?	4	4	4	4	1
14 Has water shortage led to environmental degradation?	4	4	4	4	1
15 Has underground water been affected?	4	4	4	4	4
16 Has the agricultural/agro dependent rural sector suffered due to water shortage?	1	4	4	1	1
17 Has water shortage affected domestic consumption?	1	4	4	1	4
18 Is crop diversification, or changing cropping patterns a solution to water shortage?	4	4	4	4	4
19 Is training/awareness mentioned as a solution to improve water efficiency ?	4	4	4	4	4

1: Yes
2: No
3: Ambiguous: weak assertions or difficult to comprehend
4: Not Mentioned: Query not applicable or not referred

** This is the unedited questionnaire that the main text draws on

India Spring

Article No.	01	02	03	04	05
News Paper	The Times of India	The Times of India	The Tribune	The Telegraph	The Times of India
Author	-	Dinesh K Sharma	M.S. Menon	S.L. RAO	-
Length	357	484	1336	1245	445
Type of Article	News	News	Comment	Comment	News
Date	April 02, 2010	April 03, 2010	April 04, 2010	April 05, 2010	April 06, 2010
POLITICAL DISCOURSE					
1 Are unfair/flawed provisions of IWT the reasons for water shortage?	4	4	1	4	4
2 Has regional water shortage led Pakistan to accuse India of breaching water agreements?	4	4	1	4	3
3 Have Pakistan's assertions of India not abiding by the water agreements suggested as being unreasonable?	4	4	1	4	1
4 Should Pakistan and India intensify cooperation to resolve water issues?	1	4	1	4	4
5 Has uneven inter-provincial water distribution/usage been argued to be the cause of water shortage/issue?	4	1	1	4	4
6 Has water shortage led to conflict/disagreement between stakeholders (People, Institutions, Political Parties)?	4	4	4	4	4
7 Has water been employed as a socio-political tool by extremist elements?	4	4	4	4	4
GOVERNANCE					
8 Have administrative lapses or challenges at the local, regional or national level been argued to be the cause of water shortage/issue?	4	1	1	1	1
9 Should public water management/regulation be improved to solve water shortage?	1	4	4	1	4
10 Has insufficient water/supply provision and storage infrastructure been argued to be the cause of water shortage/issue?	4	4	4	1	1
11 Will investment in water provision/technology provision and storage infrastructure reduce water shortage?	1	4	4	1	4
12 Has public-private partnership/better water pricing partnership been suggested to improve water provision?	4	4	4	4	4

Article No.	01	02	03	04	05
News Paper	The Times of India	The Times of India	The Tribune	The Telegraph	The Times of India
Author	-	Dinesh K Sharma	M.S. Menon	S.L. RAO	-
Length	357	484	1336	1245	445
Type of Article	News	News	Comment	Comment	News
Date	April 02, 2010	April 03, 2010	April 04, 2010	April 05, 2010	April 06, 2010
PEOPLE PRACTICE AND ENVIRONMENT					
13 Have changing climate/rainfall conditions caused water shortage?	4	4	4	4	4
14 Has water shortage led to environmental degradation/ issues?	4	4	4	1	4
15 Has undergound water been affected?	4	1	4	1	4
16 Has the agricultural/agro dependent rural sector suffered due to water shortage?	4	1	1	1	4
17 Has water shortage affected domestic consumption?	4	4	4	4	4
18 Is crop diversification, or changing cropping patterns a solution to water shortage?	4	4	4	4	4
19 Is training/awareness mentioned as a solution to improve water efficiency ?	4	4	4	4	4
1: Yes					
2: No					
3: Ambiguous: weak assertions or difficult to comprehend					
4: Not Mentioned: Query not applicable or not referred					
** This is the unedited questionnaire that the main text draws on					

Article No.	06	07	08	09	10
News Paper	The Hindu	The Hindu	The Indian Express	The Hindu	The Hindu
Author	Sandeep Dikshit	Afshan Yasmeen	-	Chinmaya R. Gharekhan	-
Length	492	483	166	1379	468
Type of Article	News	News	News	Feature	News
Date	April 06, 2010	April 12, 2010	April 13, 2010	April 14, 2010	April 17, 2010
POLITICAL DISCOURSE					
1 Are unfair/flawed provisions of IWT the reasons for water shortage?	4	4	4	4	4
2 Has regional water shortage led Pakistan to accuse India of breaching water agreements?	3	4	1	3	4
3 Have Pakistan's assertions of India not abiding by the water agreements suggested as being unreasonable?	1	4	4	1	4
4 Should Pakistan and India intensify cooperation to resolve water issues?	4	4	4	4	4
5 Has uneven inter-provincial water distribution/usage been argued to be the cause of water shortage/issue?	4	4	4	1	4
6 Has water shortage led to conflict/disagreement between stakeholders (People, Institutions, Political Parties)?	4	1	4	4	4
7 Has water been employed as a socio-political tool by extremist elements?	4	4	1	1	4
GOVERNANCE					
8 Have administrative lapses or challenges at the local, regional or national level been argued to be the cause of water shortage/issue?	1	1	4	1	1
9 Should public water management/Regulation be improved to solve water shortage?	4	4	4	4	4
10 Has insufficient water/supply provision and storage infrastructure been argued to be the cause of water shortage/issue?	1	1	4	1	1
11 Will investment in water provision/technology provision and storage infrastructure reduce water shortage?	4	4	4	4	1
12 Has public-private partnership/better water pricing partnership been suggested to improve water provision?	4	4	4	4	4

Article No.	06	07	08	09	10
News Paper	The Hindu	The Hindu	The Indian Express	The Hindu	The Hindu
Author	Sandeep Dikshit	Afshan Yasmeen	-	Chinmaya R. Gharekhan	-
Length	492	483	166	1379	468
Type of Article	News	News	News	Feature	News
Date	April 06, 2010	April 12, 2010	April 13, 2010	April 14, 2010	April 17, 2010

PEOPLE PRACTICE AND ENVIRONMENT

		06	07	08	09	10
13	Have changing climate/rainfall conditions caused water shortage?	4	1	4	4	4
14	Has water shortage led to environmental degradation/issues?	4	4	4	4	4
15	Has undergound water been affected?	4	1	4	4	4
16	Has the agricultural/agro dependent rural sector suffered due to water shortage?	4	4	4	4	4
17	Has water shortage affected domestic consumption?	4	1	4	4	1
18	Is crop diversification, or changing cropping patterns a solution to water shortage?	4	4	4	4	4
19	Is training/awareness mentioned as a solution to improve water efficiency ?	4	4	4	4	4

1: Yes

2: No

3: Ambiguous: weak assertions or difficult to comprehend

4: Not Mentioned: Query not applicable or not referred

** This is the unedited questionnaire that the main text draws on

Article No.	11	12	13	14	15
News Paper	The Indian Express	The Times of India	The Indian Express	The Tribune	The Indian Express
Author	-	Swati Mathur	Amitav Ranjan, Shishir Gupta	-	-
Length	459	851	482	332	453
Type of Article	News	Feature	News	News	News
Date	April 22, 2010	April 23, 2010	April 26, 2010	April 30, 2010	May 01, 2010
POLITICAL DISCOURSE					
1 Are unfair/flawed provisions of IWT the reasons for water shortage?	4	4	4	4	4
2 Has regional water shortage led Pakistan to accuse India of breaching water agreements?	4	4	1	4	3
3 Have Pakistan's assertions of India not abiding by the water agreements suggested as being unreasonable?	4	4	1	4	1
4 Should Pakistan and India intensify cooperation to resolve water issues?	4	4	3	4	4
5 Has uneven inter-provincial water distribution/usage been argued to be the cause of water shortage/issue?	4	4	4	4	4
6 Has water shortage led to conflict/disagreement between stakeholders (People, Institutions, Political Parties)?	4	4	4	4	4
7 Has water been employed as a socio-political tool by extremist elements?	4	4	4	4	4
GOVERNANCE					
8 Have administrative lapses or challenges at the local, regional or national level been argued to be the cause of water shortage/issue?	1	1	4	1	1
9 Should public water management/Regulation should be improved to solve water shortage?	4	1	4	1	4
10 Has insufficient water/supply provision and storage infrastructure been argued to be the cause of water shortage/issue?	1	1	4	4	1
11 Will investment in water provision/technology provision and storage infrastructure reduce water shortage?	4	1	4	1	4
12 Has public-private partnership/better water pricing partnership been suggested to improve water provision?	4	4	4	4	4

Article No.	11	12	13	14	15
News Paper	The Indian Express	The Times of India	The Indian Express	The Tribune	The Indian Express
Author	-	Swati Mathur	Amitav Ranjan, Shishir Gupta	-	-
Length	459	851	482	332	453
Type of Article	News	Feature	News	News	News
Date	April 22, 2010	April 23, 2010	April 26, 2010	April 30, 2010	May 01, 2010
PEOPLE PRACTICE AND ENVIRONMENT					
13 Have changing climate/rainfall conditions caused water shortage?	4	4	4	1	4
14 Has water shortage led to environmental degradation/issues?	4	4	4	4	4
15 Has undergound water been affected?	4	4	4	1	4
16 Has the agricultural/agro dependent rural sector suffered due to water shortage?	4	4	4	1	4
17 Has water shortage affected domestic consumption?	4	1	4	1	4
18 Is crop diversification, or changing cropping patterns a solution to water shortage?	4	4	4	1	4
19 Is training/awareness mentioned as a solution to improve water efficiency ?	4	4	4	1	4
1: Yes					
2: No					
3: Ambiguous: weak assertions or difficult to comprehend					
4: Not Mentioned: Query not applicable or not referred					
** This is the unedited questionnaire that the main text draws on					

Article No.	16	17	18	19	20
News Paper	The Hindustan Times	The Hindustan Times	The Indian Express	The Times of India	The Telegraph
Author	-	-	-	-	Manipadma Jena
Length	279	375	444	413	1194
Type of Article	News	News	News	News	Feature
Date	May 02, 2010	May 03, 2010	May 05, 2010	May 06, 2010	May 06, 2010
POLITICAL DISCOURSE					
1 Are unfair/flawed provisions of IWT the reasons for water shortage?	4	4	4	4	4
2 Has regional water shortage led Pakistan to accuse India of breaching water agreements?	2	1	4	4	1
3 Have Pakistan's assertions of India not abiding by the water agreements suggested as being unreasonable?	4	4	4	4	1
4 Should Pakistan and India intensify cooperation to resolve water issues?	3	4	4	4	1
5 Has uneven inter-provincial water distribution/usage been argued to be the cause of water shortage/issue?	4	4	1	4	1
6 Has water shortage led to conflict/disagreement between stakeholders (People, Institutions, Political Parties)?	4	4	3	4	4
7 Has water been employed as a socio-political tool by extremist elements?	4	4	4	4	4
GOVERNANCE					
8 Have administrative lapses or challenges at the local, regional or national level been argued to be the cause of water shortage/issue?	4	4	1	1	1
9 Should public water management/Regulation be improved to solve water shortage?	4	4	4	1	1
10 Has insufficient water/supply provision and storage infrastructure been argued to be the cause of water shortage/issue?	4	4	4	4	1
11 Will investment in water provision/technology provision and storage infrastructure reduce water shortage?	4	4	4	1	1
12 Has public-private partnership/better water pricing partnership been suggested to improve water provision?	4	4	4	4	4

Article No.	16	17	18	19	20
News Paper	The Hindustan Times	The Hindustan Times	The Indian Express	The Times of India	The Telegraph
Author	-	-	-	-	Manipadma Jena
Length	279	375	444	413	1194
Type of Article	News	News	News	News	Feature
Date	May 02, 2010	May 03, 2010	May 05, 2010	May 06, 2010	May 06, 2010
PEOPLE PRACTICE AND ENVIRONMENT					
13 Have changing climate/rainfall conditions caused water shortage?	4	4	4	4	1
14 Has water shortage led to environmental degradation/ issues?	4	4	4	4	1
15 Has undergound water been affected?	4	4	1	1	1
16 Has the agricultural/agro dependent rural sector suffered due to water shortage?	4	4	4	4	3
17 Has water shortage affected domestic consumption?	4	4	3	1	4
18 Is crop diversification, or changing cropping patterns a solution to water shortage?	4	4	4	4	3
19 Is training/awareness mentioned as a solution to improve water efficiency ?	4	4	4	4	4
1: Yes					
2: No					
3: Ambiguous: weak assertions or difficult to comprehend					
4: Not Mentioned: Query not applicable or not referred					

** This is the unedited questionnaire that the main text draws on

Article No.	21	22	23	24	25
News Paper	The Times of India	The Indian Express	The Indian Express	The Times of India	The Telegraph
Author	Nidhi Singhi	-	Tanvir A Sid-diqui	TNN	Ramachandra Guha
Length	346	424	361	419	1226
Type of Article	News	News	News	News	Comment
Date	May 06, 2010	May 10, 2010	May 10, 2010	May 19, 2010	May 22, 2010
POLITICAL DISCOURSE					
1 Are unfair/flawed provisions of IWT the reasons for water shortage?	4	4	4	4	4
2 Has regional water shortage led Pakistan to accuse India of breaching water agreements?	4	4	4	4	4
3 Have Pakistan's assertions of India not abiding by the water agreements suggested as being unreasonable?	4	4	4	4	4
4 Should Pakistan and India intensify cooperation to resolve water issues?	4	4	4	4	4
5 Has uneven inter-provincial water distribution/usage been argued to be the cause of water shortage/issue?	4	4	4	4	4
6 Has water shortage led to conflict/disagreement between stakeholders (People, Institutions, Political Parties)?	4	4	4	4	4
7 Has water been employed as a socio-political tool by extremist elements?	4	1	4	4	4
GOVERNANCE					
8 Have administrative lapses or challenges at the local, regional or national level been argued to be the cause of water shortage/issue?	1	1	1	3	1
9 Should public water management/Regulation be improved to solve water shortage?	4	4	1	1	1
10 Has insufficient water/supply provision and storage infrastructure been argued to be the cause of water shortage/issue?	4	4	4	1	4
11 Will investment in water provision/technology provision and storage infrastructure reduce water shortage?	1	4	4	3	4
12 Has public-private partnership/better water pricing partnership been suggested to improve water provision?	4	4	4	4	4

Article No.	21	22	23	24	25
News Paper	The Times of India	The Indian Express	The Indian Express	The Times of India	The Telegraph
Author	Nidhi Singhi	-	Tanvir A Siddiqui	TNN	Ramachandra Guha
Length	346	424	361	419	1226
Type of Article	News	News	News	News	Comment
Date	May 06, 2010	May 10, 2010	May 10, 2010	May 19, 2010	May 22, 2010
PEOPLE PRACTICE AND ENVIRONMENT					
13 Have changing climate/rainfall conditions caused water shortage?	4	4	4	4	4
14 Has water shortage led to environmental degradation/issues?	4	4	4	4	4
15 Has undergound water been affected?	1	4	1	1	1
16 Has the agricultural/agro dependent rural sector suffered due to water shortage?	4	4	4	4	4
17 Has water shortage affected domestic consumption?	3	4	4	1	1
18 Is crop diversification, or changing cropping patterns a solution to water shortage?	4	4	4	4	4
19 Is training/awareness mentioned as a solution to improve water efficiency ?	1	4	4	4	4

1: Yes

2: No

3: Ambiguous: weak assertions or difficult to comprehend

4: Not Mentioned: Query not applicable or not referred

** This is the unedited questionnaire that the main text draws on

Article No.	26	27	28	29	30
News Paper	The Hindu	The Hindustan Times	The Hindu	The Times of India	The Indian Express
Author	-	-	M. S. Gill	PTI	-
Length	346	439	1269	382	421
Type of Article	News	News	Feature	News	News
Date	May 25, 2010	May 26, 2010	May 28, 2010	May 28, 2010	May 30, 2010
POLITICAL DISCOURSE					
1 Are unfair/flawed provisions of IWT the reasons for water shortage?	4	4	4	4	4
2 Has regional water shortage led Pakistan to accuse India of breaching water agreements?	1	4	1	4	1
3 Have Pakistan's assertions of India not abiding by the water agreements suggested as being unreasonable?	1	4	4	4	1
4 Should Pakistan and India intensify cooperation to resolve water issues?	4	4	1	4	3
5 Has uneven inter-provincial water distribution/usage been argued to be the cause of water shortage/issue?	4	4	4	4	4
6 Has water shortage led to conflict/disagreement between stakeholders (People, Institutions, Political Parties)?	4	4	4	4	4
7 Has water been employed as a socio-political tool by extremist elements?	4	4	4	4	4
GOVERNANCE					
8 Have administrative lapses or challenges at the local, regional or national level been argued to be the cause of water shortage/issue?	4	4	1	4	1
9 Should public water management/Regulation be improved to solve water shortage?	4	4	1	1	4
10 Has insufficient water/supply provision and storage infrastructure been argued to be the cause of water shortage/issue?	4	4	1	4	4
11 Will investment in water provision/technology provision and storage infrastructure reduce water shortage?	4	4	1	1	4
12 Has public-private partnership/better water pricing partnership been suggested to improve water provision?	4	4	4	4	4

Article No.	26	27	28	29	30
News Paper	The Hindu	The Hindustan Times	The Hindu	The Times of India	The Indian Express
Author	-	-	M. S. Gill	PTI	-
Length	346	439	1269	382	421
Type of Article	News	News	Feature	News	News
Date	May 25, 2010	May 26, 2010	May 28, 2010	May 28, 2010	May 30, 2010

PEOPLE PRACTICE AND ENVIRONMENT

		26	27	28	29	30
13	Have changing climate/rainfall conditions caused water shortage?	4	4	4	1	4
14	Has water shortage led to environmental degradation/ issues?	4	4	4	4	4
15	Has undergound water been affected?	4	4	1	4	4
16	Has the agricultural/agro dependent rural sector suffered due to water shortage?	4	4	1	4	4
17	Has water shortage affected domestic consumption?	4	4	4	4	4
18	Is crop diversification, or changing cropping patterns a solution to water shortage?	4	4	1	4	4
19	Is training/awareness mentioned as a solution to improve water efficiency ?	4	4	4	1	4

1: Yes

2: No

3: Ambiguous: weak assertions or difficult to comprehend

4: Not Mentioned: Query not applicable or not referred

** This is the unedited questionnaire that the main text draws on

Article No.	31	32	33	34	35
News Paper	The Hindu	The Times of India	The Indian Express	The Hindustan Times	The Hindu
Author	Gargi Parsai	PTI	-	Zia Haq	K. Raju
Length	245	432	275	369	428
Type of Article	News	News	News	News	News
Date	May 30, 2010	May 30, 2010	June 02, 2010	June 02, 2010	June 04, 2010

POLITICAL DISCOURSE

		31	32	33	34	35
1	Are unfair/flawed provisions of IWT the reasons for water shortage?	4	4	4	4	4
2	Has regional water shortage led Pakistan to accuse India of breaching water agreements?	1	1	1	4	4
3	Have Pakistan's assertions of India not abiding by the water agreements suggested as being unreasonable?	1	1	1	4	4
4	Should Pakistan and India intensify cooperation to resolve water issues?	1	1	3	4	4
5	Has uneven inter-provincial water distribution/usage been argued to be the cause of water shortage/issue?	4	4	4	4	4
6	Has water shortage led to conflict/disagreement between stakeholders (People, Institutions, Political Parties)?	4	4	4	4	4
7	Has water been employed as a socio-political tool by extremist elements?	4	4	4	4	4

GOVERNANCE

		31	32	33	34	35
8	Have administrative lapses or challenges at the local, regional or national level been argued to be the cause of water shortage/issue?	4	4	4	4	4
9	Should public water management/Regulation be improved to solve water shortage?	4	4	4	4	4
10	Has insufficient water/supply provision and storage infrastructure been argued to be the cause of water shortage/issue?	4	4	4	4	4
11	Will investment in water provision/technology provision and storage infrastructure reduce water shortage?	4	4	4	4	4
12	Has public-private partnership/better water pricing partnership been suggested to improve water provision?	4	4	4	4	4

Article No.	31	32	33	34	35
News Paper	The Hindu	The Times of India	The Indian Express	The Hindustan Times	The Hindu
Author	Gargi Parsai	PTI	-	Zia Haq	K. Raju
Length	245	432	275	369	428
Type of Article	News	News	News	News	News
Date	May 30, 2010	May 30, 2010	June 02, 2010	June 02, 2010	June 04, 2010

PEOPLE PRACTICE AND ENVIRONMENT

	31	32	33	34	35
13 Have changing climate/rainfall conditions caused water shortage?	4	4	4	1	1
14 Has water shortage led to environmental degradation/ issues?	4	4	4	4	4
15 Has undergound water been affected?	4	4	4	4	4
16 Has the agricultural/agro dependent rural sector suffered due to water shortage?	4	4	4	1	1
17 Has water shortage affected domestic consumption?	4	4	4	4	1
18 Is crop diversification, or changing cropping patterns a solution to water shortage?	4	4	4	4	4
19 Is training/awareness mentioned as a solution to improve water efficiency ?	4	4	4	4	4

1: Yes

2: No

3: Ambiguous: weak assertions or difficult to comprehend

4: Not Mentioned: Query not applicable or not referred

** This is the unedited questionnaire that the main text draws on

Article No.	36	37	38	39	40
News Paper	The Times of India	The Hindu	The Hindu	The Indian Express	The Hindu
Author	Prabhakar Sinha & Dipak Kumar Dash	-	-	-	-
Length	333	238	327	420	240
Type of Article	News	News	News	News	News
Date	June 04, 2010	June 06, 2010	June 06, 2010	June 06, 2010	June 07, 2010

POLITICAL DISCOURSE

		36	37	38	39	40
1	Are unfair/flawed provisions of IWT the reasons for water shortage?	4	4	4	4	4
2	Has regional water shortage led Pakistan to accuse India of breaching water agreements?	4	4	4	4	4
3	Have Pakistan's assertions of India not abiding by the water agreements suggested as being unreasonable?	4	4	4	4	4
4	Should Pakistan and India intensify cooperation to resolve water issues?	4	4	4	4	4
5	Has uneven inter-provincial water distribution/usage been argued to be the cause of water shortage/issue?	4	4	4	4	4
6	Has water shortage led to conflict/disagreement between stakeholders (People, Institutions, Political Parties)?	4	4	4	4	4
7	Has water been employed as a socio-political tool by extremist elements?	4	4	4	4	4

GOVERNANCE

		36	37	38	39	40
8	Have administrative lapses or challenges at the local, regional or national level been argued to be the cause of water shortage/issue?	4	4	4	4	4
9	Should public water management/Regulation be improved to solve water shortage?	4	4	4	4	4
10	Has insufficient water/supply provision and storage infrastructure been argued to be the cause of water shortage/issue?	4	4	4	4	4
11	Will investment in water provision/technology provision and storage infrastructure reduce water shortage?	4	4	4	4	4
12	Has public-private partnership/better water pricing partnership been suggested to improve water provision?	4	4	4	4	4

Article No.	36	37	38	39	40
News Paper	The Times of India	The Hindu	The Hindu	The Indian Express	The Hindu
Author	Prabhakar Sinha & Dipak Kumar Dash	-	-	-	-
Length	333	238	327	420	240
Type of Article	News	News	News	News	News
Date	June 04, 2010	June 06, 2010	June 06, 2010	June 06, 2010	June 07, 2010

PEOPLE PRACTICE AND ENVIRONMENT

		36	37	38	39	40
13	Have changing climate/rainfall conditions caused water shortage?	4	4	4	4	1
14	Has water shortage led to environmental degradation/issues?	4	4	4	1	4
15	Has undergound water been affected?	1	4	4	1	4
16	Has the agricultural/agro dependent rural sector suffered due to water shortage?	3	4	3	4	4
17	Has water shortage affected domestic consumption?	4	4	1	4	4
18	Is crop diversification, or changing cropping patterns a solution to water shortage?	4	4	4	4	4
19	Is training/awareness mentioned as a solution to improve water efficiency ?	4	4	4	4	4

1: Yes

2: No

3: Ambiguous: weak assertions or difficult to comprehend

4: Not Mentioned: Query not applicable or not referred

** This is the unedited questionnaire that the main text draws on

	41	42	43	44	45
Article No.					
News Paper	The Hindu	The Hindu	The Indian Express	The Hindu	The Tribune
Author	T. N. Narasimhan	-	Priyadarshi Siddhanta	-	Jangveer Singh
Length	859	142	214	113	579
Type of Article	Feature	News	News	News	News
Date	June 08, 2010	June 09, 2010	June 09, 2010	June 12, 2010	June 12, 2010

POLITICAL DISCOURSE

	41	42	43	44	45
1 Are unfair/flawed provisions of IWT the reasons for water shortage?	4	4	4	4	4
2 Has regional water shortage led Pakistan to accuse India of breaching water agreements?	4	4	4	4	4
3 Have Pakistan's assertions of India not abiding by the water agreements suggested as being unreasonable?	4	4	4	4	4
4 Should Pakistan and India intensify cooperation to resolve water issues?	4	4	4	4	4
5 Has uneven inter-provincial water distribution/usage been argued to be the cause of water shortage/issue?	4	1	4	1	4
6 Has water shortage led to conflict/disagreement between stakeholders (People, Institutions, Political Parties)?	4	1	4	1	4
7 Has water been employed as a socio-political tool by extremist elements?	4	4	4	4	4

GOVERNANCE

	41	42	43	44	45
8 Have administrative lapses or challenges at the local, regional or national level been argued to be the cause of water shortage/issue?	4	3	1	4	4
9 Should public water management/Regulation be improved to solve water shortage?	1	4	4	4	4
10 Has insufficient water/supply provision and storage infrastructure been argued to be the cause of water shortage/issue?	4	4	4	4	4
11 Will investment in water provision/technology provision and storage infrastructure reduce water shortage?	1	4	4	4	4
12 Has public-private partnership/better water pricing partnership been suggested to improve water provision?	4	4	4	4	4

Article No.	41	42	43	44	45
News Paper	The Hindu	The Hindu	The Indian Express	The Hindu	The Tribune
Author	T. N. Narasimhan	-	Priyadarshi Siddhanta	-	Jangveer Singh
Length	859	142	214	113	579
Type of Article	Feature	News	News	News	News
Date	June 08, 2010	June 09, 2010	June 09, 2010	June 12, 2010	June 12, 2010

PEOPLE PRACTICE AND ENVIRONMENT

		41	42	43	44	45
13	Have changing climate/rainfall conditions caused water shortage?	1	4	4	4	4
14	Has water shortage led to environmental degradation/ issues?	4	4	4	4	4
15	Has undergound water been affected?	1	4	1	4	1
16	Has the agricultural/agro dependent rural sector suffered due to water shortage?	4	4	4	4	1
17	Has water shortage affected domestic consumption?	4	4	4	4	4
18	Is crop diversification, or changing cropping patterns a solution to water shortage?	4	4	4	4	4
19	Is training/awareness mentioned as a s a solution to improve water efficiency ?	1	4	4	4	4

1: Yes

2: No

3: Ambiguous: weak assertions or difficult to comprehend

4: Not Mentioned: Query not applicable or not referred

** This is the unedited questionnaire that the main text draws on

Article No.	46	47	48	49	50
News Paper	The Times of India	The Times of India	The Indian Express	The Telegraph	The Indian Express
Author	TNN	TNN	Ravish Tiwari	Ashok Ganguly	-
Length	276	573	1336	1616	298
Type of Article	News	Feature	Feature	Comment	News
Date	June 12, 2010	June 17, 2010	June 18, 2010	June 22, 2010	June 28, 2010
POLITICAL DISCOURSE					
1 Are unfair/flawed provisions of IWT the reasons for water shortage?	4	4	4	4	4
2 Has regional water shortage led Pakistan to accuse India of breaching water agreements?	4	4	4	4	4
3 Have Pakistan's assertions of India not abiding by the water agreements suggested as being unreasonable?	4	4	4	4	4
4 Should Pakistan and India intensify cooperation to resolve water issues?	4	4	4	4	4
5 Has uneven inter-provincial water distribution/usage been argued to be the cause of water shortage/issue?	4	1	4	1	4
6 Has water shortage led to conflict/disagreement between stakeholders (People, Institutions, Political Parties)?	4	1	4	1	4
7 Has water been employed as a socio-political tool by extremist elements?	4	4	4	4	4
GOVERNANCE					
8 Have administrative lapses or challenges at the local, regional or national level been argued to be the cause of water shortage/issue?	4	4	4	4	4
9 Should public water management/Regulation be improved to solve water shortage?	4	4	4	1	4
10 Has insufficient water/supply provision and storage infrastructure been argued to be the cause of water shortage/issue?	4	4	4	4	4
11 Will investment in water provision/technology provision and storage infrastructure reduce water shortage?	4	4	4	1	4
12 Has public-private partnership/better water pricing partnership been suggested to improve water provision?	4	4	4	1	4

	46	47	48	49	50
Article No.					
News Paper	The Times of India	The Times of India	The Indian Express	The Telegraph	The Indian Express
Author	TNN	TNN	Ravish Tiwari	Ashok Ganguly	-
Length	276	573	1336	1616	298
Type of Article	News	Feature	Feature	Comment	News
Date	June 12, 2010	June 17, 2010	June 18, 2010	June 22, 2010	June 28, 2010

PEOPLE PRACTICE AND ENVIRONMENT

		46	47	48	49	50
13	Have changing climate/rainfall conditions caused water shortage?	4	4	4	4	4
14	Has water shortage led to environmental degradation/issues?	4	4	4	4	4
15	Has undergound water been affected?	1	4	4	4	4
16	Has the agricultural/agro dependent rural sector suffered due to water shortage?	4	4	4	4	4
17	Has water shortage affected domestic consumption?	4	4	4	1	4
18	Is crop diversification, or changing cropping patterns a solution to water shortage?	4	4	4	4	4
19	Is training/awareness mentioned as a solution to improve water efficiency ?	1	4	4	4	4

1: Yes

2: No

3: Ambiguous: weak assertions or difficult to comprehend

4: Not Mentioned: Query not applicable or not referred

** This is the unedited questionnaire that the main text draws on

ARTICLE DETAILS: PAKISTAN – SPRING

	Title	Date	Publication	Type	Length	By-line
1	Generators for Wasa tubewells out-of-order	4/2/2010	The Nation	News	247	Khalid Malik
2	Citizens slam 34% hike in vegetable prices	4/5/2010	The Daily Times	News	159	-
3	Water talks	4/5/2010	The Dawn	Feature	1143	Ashfak Bokhari
4	Talks with India	4/5/2010	The Nation	Editorial	343	-
5	Environment: Mission mangroves	4/11/2010	The Dawn	Feature	841	Rehan Ali
6	Power shortage will be reduced in a month: Pervez Ashraf	4/11/2010	The Nation	News	117	-
7	Islamabad first city to have Rainwater Harvesting Programme	4/13/2010	The Daily Times	News	522	-
8	Food security: New initiatives in offering to increase agri productivity	4/14/2010	The Daily Times	News	405	-
9	Water shortage likely to deal severe blow to mango	4/15/2010	The Dawn	News	656	Mohammad Hussain Khan
10	Spot rate increases to Rs 6,300/maund	4/24/2010	The Daily Times	News	277	-
11	Power crisis dispute	4/24/2010	The Dawn	Editorial	350	-
12	Threat to mango crop	4/26/2010	The Dawn	News	625	A. B. Arisar
13	Pak wants Saarc focus on water	4/26/2010	The Nation	News	266	-
14	Pakistan for regional approach to tackle South Asian water issue	4/26/2010	The Pak Tribune	News	512	-
15	Water Issue & SAARC Summit	4/28/2010	The Pak Tribune	Feature	1242	Zaheerul Hassan
16	PM Gilani urges Saarc to ensure judicious water management Wants a common front for economic growth, against forces of extremism	4/29/2010	The Pak Tribune	News	1212	-
17	Sowing of cotton may suffer amid reduced water flow in canals	5/1/2010	The Dawn	News	467	Mansoor Mirani
18	Pakistan to move arbitration court on Kishanganga project	5/3/2010	The Dawn	Feature	686	Khaleeq Kiani
19	AJK PM on India	5/3/2010	The Nation	News	338	-
20	Water shortage cuts cotton sowing by half	5/5/2010	The Dawn	News	299	Qamaruddin
21	Saudi-Indian ties to help Pak: Envoy	5/10/2010	The Nation	News	288	-
22	Mangla filling till June 30 in doldrums	5/11/2010	Pakistan Observer	Feature	465	Shah Hasan

	Title	Date	Publication	Type	Length	By-line
23	Call for Kalabagh Dam	5/13/2010	The Nation	Editorial	382	-
24	Railway Colony protests against water shortage	5/14/2010	The Daily Times	News	78	-
25	Pindi hit by water shortage	5/14/2010	The Dawn	News	487	Aamir Yasin
26	Water supply to Thatta canals suspended	5/16/2010	The Dawn	News	364	Iqbal Khwaja
27	'Powerless' Pakistan	5/17/2010	The Dawn	Feature	816	Dr Charles K. Ebinger & Kashif Hasnie
28	CDA, WASA planning for water rationing	5/24/2010	Pakistan Observer	News	191	-
29	Lawmakers raise water shortage issue	5/25/2010	The Nation	News	233	Ramzan Chandio
30	Water crisis	5/26/2010	Pakistan Observer	Comment	147	Ghazanfar Ali Astori
31	Punjab boycotts IRSA meeting	5/26/2010	The Daily Times	News	387	Zeeshan Javaid
32	India's water hegemony	5/26/2010	The Nation	Comment	329	S.m. Hali
33	Rs31,400m for water sector	5/26/2010	The Nation	News	226	-
34	Punjab likely to contact CCI for Indus water release	5/29/2010	The Pak Tribune	News	445	-
35	Water shortage to hurt 30% standing crops in Sindh	5/30/2010	The Daily Times	News	587	Razi Syed
36	India assures Pakistan of addressing 'legitimate' water concerns	5/31/2010	The Pak Tribune	News	439	-
37	AT blames govt for Sindh's water crisis	6/1/2010	The Dawn	News	364	-
38	Pakistan, India meet over Indus waters	6/2/2010	Pakistan Observer	News	88	-
39	India violating Indus Water Treaty: FO	6/4/2010	The Nation	News	301	Kaswar Klasra
40	Agriculture sector did not perform well, says survey	6/5/2010	The Dawn	News	418	Amin Ahmed
41	India's water hegemony	6/8/2010	Pakistan Observer	Comment	1289	Lubna Umar
42	Water shortage may cripple cotton growth, experts fear	6/14/2010	The Nation	News	380	Javaid-ur-rahman
43	Farmers decry water shortage	6/15/2010	The Dawn	News	287	-
44	Deployment of Rangers at water regulator sought	6/16/2010	The Dawn	News	424	-
45	Pakistan and US agree on water sector partnership	6/18/2010	The Pak Tribune	News	225	-
46	Shortage of water triggers protests	6/19/2010	The Dawn	News	491	-
47	Rabbani asked to resolve Sindh-Balochistan water row Stresses construction of more dams	6/19/2010	The Pak Tribune	News	409	-

	Title	Date	Publication	Type	Length	By-line
48	Water availability per person down by 80.2pc	6/25/2010	Pakistan Observer	News	315	Shah Hasan
49	Sharply reducing water for citizens	6/26/2010	Pakistan Observer	Editorial	322	-
50	Population growth to reduce water availability in future	6/27/2010	The Daily Times	News	659	Ijaz Kakakhel

ARTICLE DETAILS: INDIA – SPRING

	Title	Date	Publication	Type	Length	Byline
1	It's for India, Pakistan to work out Kashmir, water issues: US	2/04/2010	The Times of India	News	357	-
2	Punjab farmers to face water crisis	3/04/2010	The Times of India	News	484	Dinesh K Sharma
3	Waters of discontent	4/04/2010	The Tribune	Comment	1336	M.S. Menon
4	FARMERS' WOES - State policies have reduced Indian agriculture to a parlous state	5/04/2010	The Telegraph	Comment	1245	S.L. RAO
5	'India didn't block water even during war'	6/04/2010	The Times of India	News	445	-
6	'Pakistan must improve storage to avoid water woes'	6/04/2010	The Hindu	News	492	Sandeep Dikshit
7	Tempers rise as water becomes scarce again	12/04/2010	The Hindu	News	483	Afshan Yasmeen
8	Next Indo-Pak war could be over water: Saeed	13/04/2010	The Indian Express	News	166	-
9	Pakistan: perceptions, prejudices & policies	14/04/2010	The Hindu	Feature	1379	Chinmaya R. Gharekhan
10	Old pipelines, leakage affect water supply in seven cities	17/04/2010	The Hindu	News	468	-
11	Water: 30-40 per cent distribution losses common in cities, says civic chief	22/04/2010	The Indian Express	News	459	-
12	Forget rural areas, even urban centres face water crisis	23/04/2010	The Times of India	Feature	851	Swati Mathur
13	PM, Gilani to hold 'limited dialogue'	26/04/2010	The Indian Express	News	482	Amitav Ranjan , Shishir Gupta
14	The water challenge	30/04/2010	The Tribune	News	332	-
15	Pakistan mismanaging Indus water: Qureshi	1/05/2010	The Indian Express	News	453	-
16	New power balance in Pak led to thaw	2/05/2010	The Hindustan Times	News	279	-
17	Pak forms legal team to take water issue with intl court	3/05/2010	The Hindustan Times	News	375	-
18	UT water hopes drying, Punjab dams supply proposal	5/05/2010	The Indian Express	News	444	-
19	Water crisis: Court asks govt to spell out strategy	6/05/2010	The Times of India	News	413	-
20	NOT A SINGLE DROP TO DRINK	6/05/2010	The Telegraph	Feature	1194	Manipadma Jena

	Title	Date	Publication	Type	Length	By- Line
21	Save 1 litre water daily, people urged	6/05/2010	The Times of India	News	346	Nidhi Singhi
22	Pak must keep option of force over water row with India: JuD	10/05/2010	The Indian Express	News	424	-
23	No law in sight to regulate groundwater extraction	10/05/2010	The Indian Express	News	361	Tanvir A Siddiqui
24	Govt mulls water supply through PPP scheme	19/05/2010	The Times of India	News	419	TNN
25	ENVIRONMENTAL CHALLENGE- Few see that India's future depends on its ecological sustainability	22/05/2010	The Telegraph	Comment	1226	Ramachandra Guha
26	India-Pakistan Water Commissioners to meet next week	25/05/2010	The Hindu	News	346	-
27	China's Himalayan plan: Dam on Brahmaputra	26/05/2010	The Hindustan Times	News	439	-
28	Water crisis of east & west Punjab	28/05/2010	The Hindu	Feature	1269	M. S. Gill
29	National Water Mission gets nod of Council on Climate Change	28/05/2010	The Times of India	News	382	PTI
30	India rubbishes Pak charges on water theft	30/05/2010	The Indian Express	News	421	-
31	Indus Water talks today	30/05/2010	The Hindu	News	245	Gargi Parsai
32	India rubbishes Pak charges on water theft	30/05/2010	The Times of India	News	432	PTI
33	Indus Water talks: Pak seeks design change in Nimmo-Bazgo	2/06/2010	The Indian Express	News	275	-
34	Climate change failed two crop cycles	2/06/2010	The Hindustan Times	News	369	Zia Haq
35	Delay in water release for irrigation	4/06/2010	The Hindu	News	428	K. Raju
36	User fee for water even in agri sector?	4/06/2010	The Times of India	News	333	Prabhakar Sinha & Dipak Kumar Dash
37	Regulatory authority for water resources?	6/06/2010	The Hindu	News	238	-
38	Signature campaign on water crisis	6/06/2010	The Hindu	News	327	-
39	'PPP model can help govt face water challenge	6/06/2010	The Indian Express	News	420	-

	Title	Date	Publication	Type	Length	By- Line
40	Conservation of water resources emphasised	7/06/2010	The Hindu	News	240	-
41	Climate council's water mission for India	8/06/2010	The Hindu	Feature	859	T. N. Narasimhan
42	Farmers seek water release	9/06/2010	The Hindu	News	142	-
43	Free power emptying Punjab groundwater: Montek	9/06/2010	The Indian Express	News	214	Priyadarshi Siddhanta
44	Punjab can't demand royalty on water: Hooda	12/06/2010	The Hindu	News	113	-
45	As water level dips, farmers' debts rise	12/06/2010	The Tribune	News	579	Jangveer Singh
46	Study of region's contour can help resolve water crisis	12/06/2010	The Times of India	News	276	TNN
47	Kishenganga water dispute: Pakistan on strong wicket	17/06/2010	The Times of India	Feature	573	TNN
48	Troubled waters	18/06/2010	The Indian Express	Feature	1336	Ravish Tiwari
49	CROSSING THE GROWTH BAR- India needs determination to go beyond the tipping point	22/06/2010	The Telegraph	Comment	1616	Ashok Ganguly
50	Pak Indus Waters Commissioner an 'Indian agent': JuD	28/06/2010	The Indian Express	News	298	-

ARTICLE DETAILS: PAKISTAN – WINTER

	Title	Date	Publication	Type	Length	Byline
1	Agriculture sector on verge of collapse: growers	1/4/2010	The Dawn	News	557	Aziz Malik
2	Indian doctrine of 'cold start' to be repelled strongly, says Kasuri	1/8/2010	The Daily Times	News	283	-
3	Govt 'apathy' over Indian water theft criticized	1/11/2010	The Dawn	News	158	-
4	India stealing Pakistan's water	1/15/2010	Pakistan Daily	Editorial	996	Sultan M Hali
5	Climate change affecting crop output, says Oxfam	1/16/2010	The Dawn	News	511	Khaleeq Kiani
6	Global War - Indian Hegemony over water	1/22/2010	The Pak Tribune	Comment	300	-
7	CDA's inefficiency main cause of water shortage	1/23/2010	The Daily Times	News	399	Mahtab Bashir
8	Quest for plan to cope with drought	1/25/2010	The Dawn	Feature	555	Khaleeq Kiani
9	Sindh Assembly session: Power plant at link canal opposed	1/29/2010	The Daily Times	News	637	-
10	Farmers fear 50pc fall in wheat production	2/1/2010	The Dawn	News	448	M.B. Kalhoro
11	FM wants bilateral resolution on Indo-Pak water crisis	2/2/2010	The Dawn	News	138	-
12	'India wants to make Kashmir issue a water conflict'	2/3/2010	The Dawn	News	115	-
13	IPCC fails to resolve Sindh-Balochistan water dispute	2/3/2010	The Pak Tribune	News	452	-
14	Pakistan on brink of mass starvation: LCCI	2/6/2010	The Nation	Comment	562	-
15	Shortage of water goes up to 34pc	2/7/2010	The Dawn	News	395	Kalbe Ali
16	PML-Q plans adjournment motions for NA session	2/8/2010	The Daily Times	News	277	-
17	MNAs seek solution to Sindh-Punjab water rift	2/10/2010	The Pak Tribune	News	596	-
18	Accord on roadmap to settle Pak-India water dispute	2/11/2010	The Dawn	News	421	Ahmad Fraz Khan

	Title	Date	Publication	Type	Length	By-line
19	Water shortage a threat to wheat crop in Sindh	2/15/2010	The Dawn	Feature	884	Saleem Shaikh
20	Water scarcity and riparian rights	2/15/2010	The Dawn	Feature	1175	Ashfak Bokhari
21	MNAs slate India for water terrorism	2/17/2010	The Nation	News	657	-
22	Pakistan to raise water issue in international forum	2/19/2010	The Dawn	News	161	-
23	Delegation ready for talks over water issue	2/19/2010	The Dawn	News	154	-
24	Water war with India?	2/20/2010	The Dawn	Comment	916	Ahmer Bilal Soofi
25	'US mediating between Pak, India to resolve water issue'	2/20/2010	The Daily Times	News	133	-
26	Water crisis deepens in lower Sindh: farmers	2/21/2010	The Dawn	News	394	Qamaruddin
27	Do they really care?	2/21/2010	The Daily Times	Comment	1261	Mohammad Ali Talpur
28	Sindh, Punjab to resolve water issue under 1991 accord	2/21/2010	The Pak Tribune	News	332	-
29	Sindh trying to resolve issue once and for all: CM	2/23/2010	The Dawn	News	565	Mohammad Hussain Khan
30	Sindh, Punjab agree on water distribution	2/23/2010	The Nation	News	312	-
31	Consensus reached: Punjab asks Irsa to stop water flow to link canal	2/23/2010	The Pak Tribune	News	388	-
32	Country's water reservoirs depleting fast	2/27/2010	The Dawn	News	364	Kalbe Ali
33	Brinkmanship to statesmanship	3/1/2010	The Nation	Comment	778	Khalid Iqbal
34	Senators want government to resolve all water issues	3/2/2010	The Daily Times	News	439	-
35	Threat to Peace - Water Ambitious India	3/3/2010	The Pak Tribune	Comment	1364	Zaheerul Hassan

	Title	Date	Publication	Type	Length	By-line
36	Future laden with hydrological warfare	3/3/2010	The Pakistan Observer	Comment	1415	Gauhar Zahid Malik
37	The looming water crisis	3/9/2010	The Dawn	Editorial	968	Ahmad Hayat
38	Thar facing acute water shortage	3/10/2010	The Dawn	Feature	721	Qurban Ali Khushik
39	Water shortage may affect sugarcane, rice crops in Kharif season	3/17/2010	The Daily Times	News	728	Ijaz Kakakhel
40	Water conservation strategy crucial	3/17/2010	The Daily Times	News	133	-
41	Govt urged to take up water issue with India	3/19/2010	The Dawn	News	303	-
42	Urgent measures to avert water crisis in Sindh urged	3/23/2010	The Dawn	News	538	-
43	The coming water disaster	3/23/2010	The Nation	Comment	853	M. Zahur-ul-Haq
44	Water problems: Alliance with friendly countries needed: Shamsul Mulk	3/26/2010	The Daily Times	News	512	-
45	Kisan Council for resolution against India	3/27/2010	The Nation	News	245	-
46	PEPCO, WAPDA squeezing the 'power' out of consumers	3/28/2010	The Daily Times	News	552	Zeeshan Javaid
47	'India not violating Indus Water Treaty'	3/28/2010	The Daily Times	News	218	-
48	Concern over water conveyed to India	3/29/2010	The Dawn	News	290	-
49	India asks Pakistan to stop blaming it for water crisis	3/29/2010	The Daily Times	News	388	Iftikhar Gilani
50	A veritable tinderbox	3/29/2010	The Nation	Comment	487	-

ARTICLE DETAILS: INDIA – WINTERS

	Title	Date	Publication	Type	Length	Byline
1	Arsenic in water may be major cause of cancer: PA	1/1/2010	The Tribune	News	537	Naveen S Garewal
2	State faces power crisis	1/7/2010	The Tribune	News	409	-
3	Thirty new waterworks to quench thirst of Mohali villages	1/9/2010	The Indian Express	News	303	-
4	Cancer Express	1/16/2010	The Hindustan Times	Feature	1202	Praveen Donthi
5	Water tariff: civil society asks for consultations across state	1/22/2010	The Indian Express	News	412	-
6	Pak pleads helplessness on attacks - Can't guarantee that 26/11 will not be repeated, Gilani tells US	1/23/2010	The Telegraph	News	447	-
7	Farmers in Lakhandur, Paoni cry for water	1/24/2010	The Times of India	Feature	597	-
8	MAKING OF A SUPERPOWER- India must do the things necessary to give its people a good life	1/25/2010	The Telegraph	Comment	1256	S.L. Rao
9	'Can't totally depend on IPCC, India to have own climate panel'	2/4/2010	The Hindustan Times	News	437	-
10	Jal Board plans ban on use of groundwater for 14 industries	2/6/2010	The Indian Express	News	372	Geeta Gupta
11	Water crisis sparks cave-in fears up north	2/8/2010	The Times of India	News	456	Prithvijit Mitra
12	Punjab rejects water bill	2/9/2010	The Tribune	News	205	-
13	Saving the day, drip by drip	2/12/2010	The Indian Express	Feature	544	Manoj Prasad
14	Water to be shifted to concurrent list	2/12/2010	The Tribune	News	527	Vibha Sharma
15	A reminder from terrorists: We don't want India-Pakistan talks	2/14/2010	The Hindu	News	518	Siddharth Varadarajan
16	Pilot water project boon to villagers	2/14/2010	The Tribune	News	291	Jangveer Singh
17	Water supply in Sirsa, Fatehabad to be augmented	2/14/2010	The Tribune	News	330	Sushil Manav
18	Pune speech on Pak soil- Glare on Lashkar front meet in Islamabad 10 days ago	2/15/2010	The Telegraph	News	457	ARCHIS MOHAN
19	Water crisis grips Kalka, Pinjore	2/23/2010	The Indian Express	News	181	Girish Sharma
20	Water Pakistan's diversionary tactic?	2/23/2010	The Times of India	News	633	-

	Title	Date	Publication	Type	Length	Byline
30	Pak muddies waters: 'don't build any power plant in J&K'	3/12/2010	The Indian Express	News	679	Ravish Tiwari
31	Severe water crisis stares Kandi areas in the face	3/12/2010	The Tribune	News	489	Dinesh Manhotra
32	Paver blocks affect groundwater levels	3/12/2010	The Hindustan Times	News	245	Bhavika Jain
33	Water shortage hits groundnut sowing in state	3/13/2010	The Indian Express	Feature	472	-
34	Pakistan for new measures to energise Indus Treaty	3/13/2010	The Hindu	News	262	Sandeep Dikshit
35	Be ready to face 35% water cut for a few days	3/16/2010	The Hindustan Times	News	114	-
36	MCC focussing on power supply to check water shortage	3/17/2010	The Times of India	News	464	-
37	Water crisis around the corner	3/17/2010	The Tribune	News	287	Neena Sharma
38	Water leakage cost govt exchequer Rs 235 crore	3/18/2010	The Times of India	News	334	Akhilesh Sourav Jha
39	Water-starved, paddy crop dying	3/18/2010	The Hindu	News	92	K. Raju
40	Parched Chas cries for water	3/18/2010	The Telegraph	News	410	SHASHANK SHEKHAR
41	City may face 35% water cut next week	3/20/2010	The Times of India	News	449	Sukhada Tatke
42	City heading for a water crisis too	3/21/2010	The Times of India	News	429	Sunil Mungara
43	Coca Cola to pay Rs 216 cr fine?	3/22/2010	The Indian Express	News	443	-
44	Tough time ahead as water crisis grips city	3/22/2010	The Times of India	News	431	P J Joychen & Akhilesh Saurav Jha
45	Arsenic-free water supply hit in Malda- Late melting of glaciers & dry spell decrease ganga flow	3/22/2010	The Telegraph	News	501	-
46	Water conservation projects a big success	3/23/2010	The Times of India	News	337	Rachna Singh
47	Cauvery water dispute back in limelight	3/23/2010	The Tribune	News	243	N Ravikumar/ TNS
48	Hanamkonda set to face water crisis	3/25/2010	The Hindu	News	316	Gollapudi Srinivasa Rao
49	TN needs sound water management to overcome scarcity: CM	3/29/2010	The Times of India	Feature	372	-
50	Land acquisition for restoring canals begins	3/31/2010	The Hindu	News	217	K. Lakshmi

www.ingramcontent.com/pod-product-compliance
Lightning Source LLC
Chambersburg PA
CBHW032353280326
41935CB00008B/556